Sir Bartle Frere

Eastern Africa as a Field for Missionary Labour

Four Letters to his Grace the Archbishop of Canterbury

Sir Bartle Frere

Eastern Africa as a Field for Missionary Labour
Four Letters to his Grace the Archbishop of Canterbury

ISBN/EAN: 9783744757362

Printed in Europe, USA, Canada, Australia, Japan

Cover: Foto ©ninafisch / pixelio.de

More available books at **www.hansebooks.com**

EASTERN AFRICA

AS A FIELD FOR

MISSIONARY LABOUR.

Four Letters

TO

HIS GRACE THE ARCHBISHOP OF CANTERBURY.

BY THE

RT. HON. SIR BARTLE FRERE, G.C.S.I., K.C.B., D.C.L.,

MEMBER OF THE INDIAN COUNCIL, AND PRESIDENT OF THE
ROYAL GEOGRAPHICAL SOCIETY.

WITH A MAP.

LONDON:
JOHN MURRAY, ALBEMARLE STREET.
1874.

[*Right of Translation reserved.*]

By the same Author.

THE BENGAL FAMINE. How it will be Met, and How to Prevent Future Famines in India. With 3 Maps. Crown 8vo. 5s.

RESULTS OF INDIAN MISSIONS. *Third Edition.* Small 8vo. 2s. 6d.

"A very important contribution to the history and prospects of missionary enterprise in Hindostan."—*Scotsman.*

"This very interesting essay."—*Record.*

"Sir Bartle Frere's work is highly valuable for the information which it gives, and as containing the testimony of one eminently entitled to be listened to with respect."—*Edinburgh Courant.*

"Sir Bartle Frere gives a most interesting account of the progress of mission work in India."—*Daily Review.*

CONTENTS.

	PAGE
INTRODUCTORY ..	7

FIRST LETTER :—

Great Field for Missionary Labour on East African Coast ..	9
Classes of Population	10
I. Foreigners	10
Europeans	10
Americans and Asiatics	10
Arabs	10
Indians	10
II. African Races of Mixed Descent	11
1. Swahili, Inhabitants of Coast ..	11
2. Gallas	11
3. Somalis	12
4. Comoro Islanders	12
III. Negro Races ..	13
Languages	13
Philological Works and Translations, completed or in progress	14
Existing Religions	14
Fetish Superstition of Negro Races—Position of its disciples in relation to Christianity	15

Contents.

FIRST LETTER (*continued*):—

	PAGE
Christianity of former days	16
Islam	17
Numbers of various Races within reach of Missionaries from the Coast	20

SECOND LETTER:—

Missionary Agencies now at work	22
Roman Catholic Mission at Aden	23
Universities' Mission at Zanzibar and Magila ..	24
French Mission at Zanzibar and Bagamoyo	48
Church Missionary Society's Mission at Mombassa and Kissoludini	59
Mission of United Methodists' Free Churches at Ribe ..	60
Other Stations suggested as suitable for Missionary Establishments	63
Portuguese Clergy at Ibo and Mozambique	66
French Priests at Mayotte and Nossi Bé	66
Native Malagash Church at Majunga, in Madagascar	66
Comoro Islands	68

THIRD LETTER:—

Recapitulation as to work to be done on the East Coast of Africa	69
Ideal pattern of a completely organised Christian Mission to uncivilised races	70
Practice of the early Church in dealing with uncivilised communities	71
Departure from that practice in many of the Missionary Societies of the Reformed Churches in the eighteenth and nineteenth centuries	71

Contents.

THIRD LETTER (*continued*):—

	PAGE
Adherence of others to the primitive practice	72
Principle that in Christian Missions nothing should be neglected which is necessary to the organisation of a perfectly civilised Christian Society	73
Necessary prominence of clerical element	74
Branches in which lay element may be most useful	74
Medical Missionaries	75
A certain amount of medical training should be required in all missionaries	75
Exclusively Medical Missionaries—their School and College Training	76
Nurses	80
Philologists and Scholars	80
Teachers and Schoolmasters	81
Printers	81
Artisans, Mechanics, and Agriculturists	83
Note.—The "General Instructions" of the S. P. G., and of the London Missionary Society	85

FOURTH LETTER:—

Means of supplying what is wanted by Missions in Eastern Africa	94
Terms of engagement for Missionaries, clerical and lay	95
Questions of Celibacy of Agents employed	96
Objection on score of expense: Answered	97
Selection of Agency	99
Connection of each Mission with special localities in our own country	100
Raising of Funds	101

FOURTH LETTER (*continued*):—

	PAGE
Connection of Missions with University Life, and studies of Churchmen	102
Example: study of Semitic Languages	103
Canon Westcott's suggestions	105
Direct connection between misbelief or unbelief in Christendom, with the varying forms of Religion and Philosophy in Heathendom	107
Aid to be derived from India. C. M. S.'s African Orphanage at Nassick. Free Church Institution, Bombay	107
General Missionary Library in England	113
Co-operation of different Missionary Societies in this and similar undertakings	114
Application of principles above stated to Missions in East Africa	114
Opinions of Dr. Steere	115
Conclusion	117

The MAP *of* EAST AFRICA *to be placed at the end.*

INTRODUCTORY.

TO HIS GRACE THE ARCHBISHOP OF CANTERBURY.

MY DEAR LORD ARCHBISHOP,

These pages have grown out of a letter I began writing to your Grace on board H.M.S. *Enchantress*, on the East Coast of Africa, descriptive of what had been seen and heard by the late Mission to Zanzibar, of a nature likely to be of special interest to you as Metropolitan of our Established National Church.

I submit them simply as a collection of notes and suggestions, certain that anything they may contain likely to be useful will be applied in whatever way you may think best calculated to promote the preaching of the Gospel among the races of Eastern Africa.

I make no apology for anything I have said regarding other branches of Christ's Church which are not in direct communion with our own; partly because I know that everything connected with any section of the Church at large interests you personally; but more because—

in the presence of the great superstitions which keep those lands in intellectual and moral darkness, and which degrade such vast portions of mankind to the level of the beasts that perish—the differences of discipline or of dogma which divide us so sharply here at home, are so dwarfed that all seem to fight under one banner. I met in Africa few who would not gladly welcome, as a brother and fellow-labourer, any one who came to work alongside them in the spirit which your Grace has always manifested in dealing with sincere Christians, though they may be here unhappily divided from us by sectarian or doctrinal differences; and I feel sure that many who in this country might scruple to acknowledge your authority, further than as by human law established, would gladly, if the means of doing so offered, take counsel with you and of you regarding matters of eternal moment to Africa; and would on those shores recognise, as moved by the Holy Ghost, any teachers who you may send forth animated by the same spirit of Christian love and catholic charity which has directed your Grace's dealings with all who bear the name of Christ in these lands.

I remain, with sincere respect,
Your Grace's faithful and obedient Servant,

H. B. E. FRERE.

FIRST LETTER.

Great Field for Missionary Labour on East African Coast.
Classes of Population.
  I. Foreigners:—
    Europeans.
    Americans and Asiatics.
    Arabs.
    Indians.
  II. African Races of Mixed Descent:—
    1. Swahili, Inhabitants of Coast.
    2. Gallas.
    3. Somalis.
    4. Comoro Islanders.
  III. Negro Races:—
    Languages.
    Philological Works and Translations, completed or in progress.
    Existing Religions.
    Fetish Superstition of Negro Races—Position of its Disciples in relation to Christianity.
    Christianity of former days.
    Islam.
    Numbers of various Races within reach of Missionaries from the Coast.

It would be difficult to find elsewhere so wide or so favourable a field for missionary labour as the East African coast and islands present at this moment, from the mouth of the Red Sea to the Portuguese frontier near Cape Delgado, in lat. 11° S., and including the Comoro and other islands off that coast. In no other country that I know do *artificial* obstacles to success appear so small; and there are probably few parts of any continent where so little has been hitherto done by Christian nations to pre-occupy the ground.

II.

The races which are more entirely African, either by origin or by having become permanently rooted in the soil, may be classed as:—

1. Swahili, or coast tribes, in whom the foreign element, chiefly Arab or Persian, is most marked. They have much landed and territorial influence on the islands and seashore, and speak generally one language—African in construction and modes of inflection, &c., but abounding in Arabic and other foreign words and idioms. It is readily learnt; possesses great capacity for adopting from other languages what it does not possess in itself; is universally current along the whole line of coast, and forms an easy introduction to other more purely African tongues.

The Swahili seems admirably adapted as a general language for the coast, especially useful to strangers as a first language to acquire.

Distinct from the Swahili we find a number of African tribes with a great, but very ancient northern, possibly Arab or Ethiopic, admixture, e. g. :—

2. Gallas—a people of mixed race, with many varieties of type; some obviously Negroid, others men of large frame and light brown colour, who might pass for Egyptians or Arabs, but for a height of cheek-bone and squareness of forehead which are more characteristic of Northern European than of Southern Caucasian or Semitic races. They are more pastoral in their habits than most of the purely Negro tribes. They have a soft, flexible, and copious language, which has been reduced to writing by Christian missionaries in Abyssinia, and is easily acquired. Books have been printed in it by the German missionaries at Ankobar, the capital of Shooa, the southern-

most kingdom of Abyssinia. The Gallas seem at one time to have nearly enveloped the southern, south-eastern, and south-western portions of Abyssinia, and to have been an aggressive and conquering race; but of late years they have been much pressed on and enfeebled by their neighbours, and except on the south, between Mombassa and Lamoo, they have nearly been excluded from the sea-coast. The Northern Gallas are for the most part nominal Muhammedans; the Southern generally retain some form of old African superstition.

Among their most dreaded neighbours are—

3. Somalis—tribes of which people occupy the whole coast from about the mouth of the Red Sea to near Lamoo, in lat. 2° S. Physically, they are not unlike the higher types of Galla, but with more Arab admixture both in form and language; generally nominal Muhammedans, pastoral in their habits; an energetic, passionate, wild, and uncultivated people, but with many good qualities, and fair capacity for learning. Till lately they have been often described as irreclaimable savages; but since the occupation of Aden they have flocked thither in great numbers as labourers and out-of-door servants, in which capacity they have won for themselves a very fair character from their European employers.

4. The Comoro Islanders are few in number, but important from their intelligence and position. There are many varieties of race—some very large and handsome, and others small and debased. There is, perhaps, in all an admixture of Malagash or Malay, as well as Arab and Persian and Negro blood.

III.

We have the pure Negro races: infinite in variety of form, from the typical black gigantic Ethiop—such as he is described in romances, and more rarely seen among the tribes of the far interior—down to types little superior to Cape Bushmen.

Between extreme specimens of each tribe it is easy to see distinctions so marked, that there seems at first no difficulty in classifying them; but further experience shows that anything like classification by tribes from external physical characteristics is difficult in the presence of a gradation in the form of every limb and feature, denoting races more intermixed than in most other countries.

This may be partly owing to social habits, such as slavery, polygamy, and the like; but more, perhaps, to long-continued political disorder and disintegration. Weak tribes are absorbed by strong ones, powerful races are enfeebled by extended conquest and by the absorption of inferior clans, till the original types become hardly distinguishable. The confusion is rendered greater by the utter absence of literature, or of history reaching much further back than living memory, and by a prevalent child-like inaccuracy of observation in all that does not affect the physical wants of the individual.

Varieties of language will, no doubt, hereafter assist classification, when we know more about them. At present, besides the Swahili, or coast language, already alluded to, there appear to be at least five or six well-marked types of language to be met within two hundred miles of the seashore between the Gallas and the Portuguese frontier;

but every scholar who studies these tongues seems to take a different view as to whether the specific differences already recognised are too many, or whether the distinct languages hitherto ascertained do not require further subdivision. Probably more of them must be carefully analysed and reduced to writing before any final and decisive judgment on such points can be formed.

Meanwhile, if the dictionaries already prepared by the Rev. Mr. Rebmann, of the Church Missionary Society, long resident at Kissoludini and Mombassa, could be printed, they would prove of the greatest value to future scholars. They are said to be complete as regards the Swahili, Nyassa, and Wanika languages, and their publication will mark an era in modern African philology.

The labours of Dr. Steere, of the Universities' Mission at Zanzibar, have already rendered it easy to acquire as much of Swahili as is needed for practical mission work, and have greatly facilitated the study of three other dialects (Shambala, Nyamwesi, and Yao); and, if he is spared to continue the work, I have little doubt that it will, at no distant period, be in the power of a missionary to obtain, in a few months, a fair colloquial acquaintance with the speech of any of the tribes near the coast along the whole line of the Zanzibar territory. The great work of translating the Holy Scriptures into East African languages will then still remain to be undertaken.

Hitherto there are in print only single books of Holy Scripture, and a few selected portions translated by Drs. Krapf, Rebmann, and Steere, into Northern Galla, Wanika, and Swahili.

With the exception of Muhammedanism, which is here, as elsewhere in Africa, an advancing and converting faith, nowhere on the East Coast does there seem to be any very strong pre-occupation of the ground by any powerful dominant superstition or religion. There is little idolatry or fetish-worship such as is found on the West Coast, and few barbarous or unnatural rites. A childish vacancy of belief, and materialism more or less marked; seem the general characteristics of the religion, if religion it can be called, of the principal tribes. There is great difficulty in getting them to apprehend any kind of abstract idea or to realize any non-physical agency.

Intelligent men usually admit the existence of a Great Spirit, who, however, they believe does not much concern himself with human affairs. There is generally some misty notion of the immortality of the soul and of a hereafter, but the present is the only thing they deem really worth thinking of; physical good and evil are, they believe, dependent on natural self-existent laws of being, remotely affected by inferior spiritual natures who are worked on by charms, and who communicate with mankind by portents. These are understood, and the beings from whom they emanate may be influenced in some degree by the initiated. People wiser than their neighbours can always by spiritual agency work some good or evil, inflicting or curing sickness, bad harvests, drought, &c.; but all the popular notions of the agency by which good or evil are worked are very indistinct. The subject is not one which appears to have much hold on the minds of the people in general. In some tribes, as the Wanika, there are powerful initiated classes, and forms of initiation which are only gone through after long probation, and a great expenditure in eating and drinking. The body of initiated have considerable temporal power, and decide in secret council on all important matters affecting the tribe. But the organisation apparently more resembles that of an eating and drinking club than of a religious or political body, and the greatest secret seems to be the whereabouts and mode of beating a huge drum, which is kept in a remote spot in the forest, and whose sounds inspire a certain amount of awe. The whole belief, as far as I could ascertain, is more like children playing at bogies than the sanguinary superstitions of the Guinea Coast.

The doctrines of Christianity to such people are new truths—"possibly," as they might put it, "very good in their way, like the knowledge of the ingredients of gunpowder or the art of ship-building," but not visibly antagonistic to any old belief; "the power of spells and omens being," they would say, "as much matter of fact and experience as the action of quinine."

It is obvious that in dealing with such a people the process must be essentially different from that of converting people who have a definite religion such as the Hindoos.

The Africans have, so to speak, no fixed belief, but a multitude of bad habits and baseless fears. They have absolutely no inheritance of knowledge, either in morals or creeds, but ample power to acquire such knowledge when presented to them; and the few who have a chance of profiting by European or Asiatic education seem quite as apt scholars as the ordinary run of children in other continents.

It is curious how little trace is now to be found of the Christian missions established on these shores in former days. When the Portuguese first visited them, there were still some communities of Syrian Christians, and we hear of Syrian bishops—Socotra being one of the sees. Hardly a tradition of these earlier Christian communities is now to be found on the spot where they once flourished. The Portuguese conquerors gave large grants to their clergy, and built numerous and magnificent churches, some of the ruins of which still remain. These and a few forts are almost the only evidences to be found of former Portuguese dominion north of Cape Delgado. I could not learn that they had left any native converts behind them in the territories from which they have been expelled during the last century, and their policy in matters connected with religion seems to have differed little from that followed in their civil and military administration, which has left an evil repute behind them on all the coast they formerly possessed. Happily for modern missionaries, the religion they preach seems seldom identified in the minds of their present hearers with that professed by the early Portuguese conquerors.

As regards Islam, there can be no doubt it spreads wherever the Arabs go. It is a great step in advance, as compared with the indigenous native African superstitions, and tends to raise its converts in the social as well as the moral scale. But it does not appear to me that in East Africa, any more than in India or Egypt, it is an advancing religion in the same sense or to the same degree as Christianity. From a variety of causes there has been during the last generation a kind of revival, which has multiplied the missionaries of Islam, and they have much success wherever the ground is unoccupied or feebly held by any other creed. But where the Moslem preachers are most learned and energetic, despair rather than hope seems, as far as my observation extends, to be their predominant motive, and their enthusiasm and such success as they achieve remind one more of the flicker of the expiring flame than the steady brilliancy of earlier victories. Certainly their progress in these days is greatest where there is least mental, commercial, or political activity. The whole current of modern thought and inquiry is against them, and it is daily becoming more difficult for the Moslem student to find any field of intellectual exercise to which he can devote himself without risk to his orthodoxy, save in the somewhat over-cultivated regions of the critical exegesis of his sacred text and traditions. Even then, unless warily kept to the ancient paths, he may find the received creed regarding the Prophet and his mission rudely shaken by the results of his historical inquiries.

But it is only when he comes in contact with Western thought and modes of inquiry that the Moslem enthusiast incurs this risk. Among the uncivilised Negro tribes he may always be sure of a ready audience; he can not only give them many truths regarding God and man which make their way to the heart and elevate the intellect, but he can at once communicate the Shibboleth of admission to a social and political communion, which is a passport for protection and assistance from the Atlantic to the Wall of China. Wherever a Moslem house can be found, there the Negro convert who can repeat the dozen syllables of his creed, is sure of shelter, sustenance, and advice; and in his own country he finds himself at once a member of an influential, if not of a dominant caste.

This seems to me the real secret of the success of the Moslem missionaries in West Africa. It is great and rapid as regards numbers, for the simple reason that the Moslem missionary, from the very first profession of the convert's belief, acts practically on those principles regarding the equality and brotherhood of all believers before God, which Islam shares with Christianity; and

as a Field for Missionary Labour. 19

he does this, as a general rule, more speedily and decidedly than the Christian missionary, who generally feels bound to require good evidence of a converted heart before he gives the right hand of Christian fellowship, and who has always to contend with race prejudices not likely to die out in a single generation where the white Christian has for generations been known as master, and the black heathen as slave.

Making every allowance for the advantage thus given to the missionary of Islam in that particular region, the descriptions we have lately read of the great progress of Islam as compared with Christianity seem to me to require confirmation. They generally, as far as I have read them, strike me as insensibly exaggerated in consequence of the writer's surprise at finding the Muhammedan convert anything better than an utterly untutored savage.

But whatever may be the case with regard to the West Coast, there can, I think, be no doubt that on the East Coast, as in India and elsewhere, the Muhammedan religion bears all the marks of a decaying creed, which has no chance of success in propagating itself save among a people but little removed from barbarism; and that as an aggressive growing religion, capable of making conquests in civilised as well as uncivilised communities, its power cannot be compared to that exhibited in our own day by Christianity.

I am not insensible of a certain amount of acceptance which Muhammedanism finds nowadays among a few classes of our own countrymen : with some the convenience of its moral doctrines has a charm ; with others the severe simplicity of its creed, and the vigour of its early practice. A love of eccentricity influences some, and there is a very considerable amount of real sympathy with decaying greatness which lends a sentimental kind of halo to an unpractical admiration for doctrines connected with much of romance and stirring history.

The few vigorous thinkers who manifest an admiration for the Muhammedan system seem to be led away by its worship of a God of force. Energy and success may for a time blind us to the real characteristics of the creed as a foundation for a moral or a political system; but a closer acquaintance with its practical results must, I think, convince the unbiassed inquirer that it is a creed fatal in the long run to human progress and human happiness, and that it bears within itself the seeds of that inevitable decay which is every day becoming more manifest in the regions where it has been longest the dominant creed.

It would be impossible to give anything approaching to accurate statistics of any of the various races referred to above as making up the population between the Red Sea and the Portuguese frontier. The following figures are, in most cases, little better than plausible guesses of the number of each class which may be within reach of missionaries from the East African coast. In the case of the larger indigenous tribes it is quite possible that the true numbers may be double those here given; but in no case do I think they are over-estimated:—

1. Europeans and Americans, only a few individuals at the principal ports.

2. "Banians" and others of Indian origin, 7000 or 8000.

3. Arabs and persons of distinct Arab or Persian descent, roughly estimated at about ten times the number of Indians—say, 70,000 or 80,000, of whom probably not more than a tithe are of pure Arab descent.

4. Somalis. The whole race has been estimated at four or five millions; perhaps one million may be within reach of the East Coast.

5. Gallas. The aggregate estimate of the various tribes gives double the total of the Somalis; but probably less than a million are within reach of East Coast missions.

6. Negro population, on a strip 100 to 150 miles wide inland from the sea, roughly calculated at from fifteen to twenty-two souls per square mile, are set down at from four to five millions. From what I saw of the coast population I should think this very much under the mark.

SECOND LETTER.

Missionary Agencies now at work.
Roman Catholic Mission at Aden.
Universities' Mission at Zanzibar and Magila.
French Mission at Zanzibar and Bagamoyo.
Church Missionary Society's Mission at Mombassa and Kissoludini.
Mission of United Methodists' Free Churches at Ribe.
Other Stations suggested as suitable for Missionary Establishments.
Portuguese Clergy at Ibo and Mozambique.
French Priests at Mayotte and Nossi Bé.
Native Malagash Church at Majunga, in Madagascar.
Comoro Islands.

I will now briefly describe the Christian Missions which we found existing and devoting themselves especially to the conversion of the natives of the East African coast. I will not attempt to recapitulate what Livingstone and the travellers who have followed him have done to prepare the way for missionaries. Livingstone's work was avowedly and intentionally missionary, and wherever he has gone, he has, like John the Baptist, prepared the way for the Gospel; he has preached the advent of Him who should bring " good tidings to the meek, proclaim liberty to the captives, and opening of the prison to them that are bound;" and wherever missionaries follow him, they will find the message they bear recognised as that of which Livingstone spoke. But I will here confine myself to briefly enumerating the various mission stations which are already in existence and maintained by various churches on these coasts.

Eastern Africa.

The following extracts from an official report on the subject of the disposal of liberated slaves* describe the missionary agencies now at work.

At Aden the only mission in active operation is maintained by the Roman Catholics, chiefly as a base of operations for their missions in the Abyssinian kingdom of Shooa. There is an African orphanage, which is thus described in a memorandum by Major Euan Smith, private secretary to the Envoy:—

"The Lady Prioress of the Convent of the Good Shepherd states that in 1868–69 the convent first began to receive released slaves from Government, and that it is 'principally for them that the nuns of the "Good Shepherd" now remain in Aden.' The convent could not now give accommodation to more than fifty children, including those at present under its charge—eleven in number; should Government wish to place a larger number under their charge, a school would have to be built for them. The average cost of each child per annum is stated to be 7*l.*, but the nuns would gladly receive all children for 5*l.* per head per annum, trusting to the child to earn the rest.

"The instruction given to the children is in reading, writing, and religion, and also sewing and household work generally. The children remain with the nuns until married or placed in service, but 'those who wish to remain are never forced to leave.' Their age, when received, varies from six to eleven, and though morose and apathetic at first, they soon improve under the influence of kind treatment, and prove themselves, with few exceptions, tractable and intelligent.

"The Préfet Apostolique of the Roman Catholic Mission at Aden also expresses his desire to 'form an establishment at Aden, composed entirely of liberated slaves, who would be brought up to different trades, such as masons, carpenters, shoemakers, tailors, bookbinders,' &c. For the moment, he says that

---

* Correspondence respecting mission to the East Coast of Africa, 1872-3. Presented to Parliament, 1873. Pp. 121-127.

' accommodation could only be afforded for thirty, but after a short time a much larger number might be taken, as a school is already built, and will be vacant after some months.' The Reverend Father adds that the terms on which the boys would be received are similar to those which the nuns consider necessary for the girls, i.e. 5*l*. per annum.

"These two establishments afford an excellent asylum for liberated slave children at a very moderate rate; and they might very conveniently be made use of for slaves taken by our cruisers within the neighbourhood of Aden. The rate demanded for the children seems small, and they are certain to receive kind and liberal treatment at the hands of the Brethren and Sisters.

"In the case of slaves remaining at either establishment until grown up and able to earn their own livelihood, the Government rate should be reduced in proportion as the slave was able to work for himself.

"It may be added that, on the inspection of the slave children by Sir Bartle Frere on his way to Zanzibar in January 1873, all appeared healthy, happy, and contented; the advantages offered by the care of the Sisters and Brethren, the salubrity of Aden itself, and the absolute security assured to the liberated slave, together with the facility of supervision which might be exercised, if necessary, by the Government authorities, are strong arguments for the establishment of a small settlement of liberated slaves at Aden."

At Zanzibar we find—

I. THE UNIVERSITIES' MISSION.

"The Universities' Mission was originally organized by Bishop Mackenzie in 1860 as a mission to the tribes of Shire and Lake Nyassa. Its head-quarters were established by his successor, Bishop Tozer, in 1864, at Zanzibar, where they have now commodious mission-houses, schools, two small plots of ground for cultivation, and a printing-press.

"On the mainland they have, at Magila, a small house and plot of land, in charge of a native catechist, a long day's journey inland from Morongo, a small port north of the

Pangani River. The station is in the district called Mtangata in the Usambara country, in the territory of a native chief who considers himself independent of Zanzibar. It is capable of indefinite extension, and is extremely well placed for communication with the interior.

"The missionaries have laboured at Zanzibar to train selected lads for school teaching and for pastoral missionary work, giving, for this purpose, a good deal of attention to both English and the native languages.

"In both respects they have been successful; a fair proportion of the pupils have a useful knowledge of English, and all have learned to read and write their own language, or at least Swahili, the general language of the coast, in English character, in a manner which has hardly been attempted by other missions, and which leaves little to be desired.

"This is mainly due to the labours of Dr. Steere, which are more fully described below. He has furnished any one who can read English with the means of thoroughly mastering Swahili, the most generally useful of East African languages, and greatly facilitated the acquisition of three others commonly spoken by slaves.

"Very excellent work, in these languages and in English, is turned out at the Mission-press, the whole being composed, set up, and printed off by negro lads and young men.

"It is difficult to overestimate the value of Dr. Steere's labours in these two branches of mission-work; and nothing more seems wanting in either, than to continue and extend what has been so well begun.

"In the benefits of both, as most important auxiliaries in the suppression of the Slave Trade, and in the general civilisation of East Africa, the Government partly participates. It is to this Mission also that we must, for the present, mainly look for a supply of well-educated interpreters, able to read and write both English and Swahili.

"Judged as a whole, for secular purposes, such as the disposal of liberated slaves, the main defect of the Mission seems to me to be the want of more industrial teaching in mechanical arts or agriculture; many even of the best-selected lads have absolutely no capacity for intellectual acquirement by means of reading or writing, and I have heard of what were called 'lamentable failures,' so called simply because a boy who was quite willing to work in the fields for his living, but had no capacity for any but bodily exercises, ran away from his lessons.

"If I might presume to advise the Bishop and the missionaries, I would introduce a far larger industrial element into their schools. Every one should learn a trade or mechanical art of some kind, or sufficient of agriculture to support himself. The teaching might be such as a good native artisan, or mechanic or cultivator, could impart—to which might be added tentatively, and with caution, instruction in European methods and the use of European tools, which are not invariably adapted to African habits and necessities. Every boy should, I think, be taught to make himself useful in building a hut, in cultivating, in managing a boat or fishing-canoe, washing, making, and mending his own clothes and shoes, and his nets and fishing-tackle, &c., after the native fashion, with European improvements only when clearly seen to be better than the native ways.

"Elementary instruction sufficient to read and write in their own language might probably be imparted to all: but only the apter pupils should be required to learn English.

"There is room for something being done in this way on the ground which Bishop Tozer has already acquired, but more space is needed and might be acquired on the island or on the mainland, if the plans for extension which the Mission has in view can be carried out.

"On the island it might be found in a small 'shamba' or plantation, such as the Consul would have to provide for the temporary reception of any batch of liberated slaves which might be brought in, pending adjudication or awaiting distribution. The Consul, instead of himself undertaking the maintenance of such a plantation, might make it over to be managed by the Mission, if the latter were able to undertake it, and the arrangement might be made an economical one for both parties.

"Nothing could be better placed, for all the purposes which Government has in view, than the missionary outpost at Magila, on the borders of the Usambara country. But unless Mr. Allington, the missionary who selected the station, should return, the Mission must be strengthened, and some time must elapse before it would be safe to send thither liberated slaves.

"The same may be said of Dar-es-Salaam, about midway between the delta of the Lufiji and the delta of the Kingani, near Bagamoyo—to the occupation of which, as a station on the mainland, the attention of the Universities' Mission has been for some time directed.

"In its present state, this Mission could take charge of a considerable number of children at Zanzibar, if they were gradually added to the present charge; and I understand from Dr. Steere that almost any number which is likely to offer could be taken in charge, if some notice were given to prepare for their reception."

While at Zanzibar I put some queries to Dr. Steere, and he was kind enough, in reply, to give me the following information :—

"1. The Universities' Mission has had under its care, since its arrival in Zanzibar, 78 boys and 32 girls, in all 110 children; of these, all, except five boys, were released slaves. Fourteen of the boys were taken out of slave-dhows by Seyyid Majid, and put by him under the care of the Mission; two boys and one girl were procured by Europeans (not British subjects) residing in Zanzibar, and given over by them to the Mission; the rest were all taken by English men-of-war. Nineteen children have died; three of the girls are married; two of the boys are sub-deacons—one is at the Magila mission station, the other is preparing to go there : one old scholar is chief assistant in the printing-office, another is employed about the Mission premises, one is engaged as servant to Bishop Tozer, four are in service in the town of Zanzibar, three are engaged as pupil teachers in the school, four have in various ways turned out badly. Forty-two boys and twenty-two girls are now in the schools.

"2. The cost of maintenance has been calculated at 6*l.* a year, which has hitherto been amply sufficient; prices are, however, continually rising, and living is perceptibly more expensive than it was a few years ago.

"3. The liberated slaves under the charge of the Mission have been taught the ordinary subjects of primary education, including the English language. They are lodged in the Mission houses, and their conduct has generally been very good. The boys are now printing some elementary school-books in Swahili, as it is desirable that all should learn and be able to teach in that language, while only those who show some special aptitude need be taught English or any other language.

"4. One piece of ground was till lately occupied by the two sub-deacons, who made some profit out of it—I cannot say to what extent. Various attempts have been made on a small scale, but the land near the school-house is exceedingly infertile, and that at Mbweni, which is very good, is not conveniently situated in regard to the boys' school. Bishop Tozer purchased it with a view to planting out upon it adult released slaves, but none were ever actually received. It must be observed that the object of our schools was to train missionaries, and only indirectly for the benefit of released slaves.

"5. Land can only be purchased in Zanzibar from time to time as opportunity offers. There is no great stretch of fertile land which is not already occupied, and many of the native owners are exceedingly unwilling to sell to European purchasers. I do not think that any colony of released slaves could be planted in the Island of Zanzibar itself with a reasonable prospect of success.

"6. The Mission boys do the work of the house, keep the land in order, so far as their other occupations allow, and work the printing-press. They have several times been employed in carpentering work under a European teacher, but never with much success, owing partly to failures in health and other defects in the teachers, and partly to the fact that European tools and methods are not very well adapted to native habits and wants. The fact is that, except for supplying the wants of European residents, European or Europeanizing mechanics are not wanted at all. Our Mission has always aimed at keeping natives still in native dress and habits.

"7. The Universities' Mission is at present represented by myself, and I have more to do than I can properly attend to. To speak frankly, I think our proper work is among the heathen in their own homes, and not among released slaves. If our friends at home wish it, and will send out two or three competent men, I think a settlement of released slaves might be formed somewhere on the mainland under authority, and on land granted by Seyyid Burgash; and I should suggest Dar-es-Salaam as a good situation. It would be necessary to maintain all persons landed there until their first crop was ready for use. At present I should be glad to take in ten or twenty girls more, but I had rather not have any increase in the number of our boys.

"8. Our station at Magila is intended as a point of departure for preaching amongst the Shambala. It is a long day's journey inland, nearly opposite the middle of the Island of Pemba. Permission to settle there was given by the then King of the Shambala to the Rev. C. A. Allington. The Mission has no definite property, except the houses actually occupied by its members. There is land capable of use for pasturage and for growing corn, but nearly all of it is already occupied. The soil is, I believe, fertile, the natives friendly, and the climate at least as good as that of Zanzibar. The Government is very unsettled; a war of disputed succession has been going on for ten or twelve years among the Shambala, and is not yet ended, though just now there is a sort of truce arising from the exhaustion of the country generally. The access from the coast is as easy as on most usual roads, but not at all specially so; and any large settlement of released slaves would, I feel sure, be regarded by all parties with great suspicion. I ought to mention that I have never seen Magila, and therefore only speak from what I have heard from those who have visited it. I think that

Dar-es-Salaam is the only spot near Zanzibar which offers any special advantages for a new settlement, but I believe that there are many eligible places to the south of Kilwa. From the little I have seen of that coast, I should expect it to prove healthy, but rather barren. I have seen very little really fertile land in Eastern Africa, and I think its general fertility has been very much exaggerated. I think any convenient harbour under British Government would very soon draw away the trade from Zanzibar, and become the emporium of Eastern Africa. I think that in most places released slaves would be able to get food for themselves after a season or two. I think that they would soon increase and improve under any regular Government; but I do not think that European methods could be rapidly introduced, unless under some system of modified slavery. I think Negroes are most out of the reach of the slave-dealer when residing on the coast. It would be impossible to hold any district of the country as free soil at a distance in the interior without a strong European force. It must be remembered that there is a Slave Trade into the interior as well as to the coast."

Dr. Steere subsequently forwarded to me copies of some of his Reports to the Committee of the Mission in England, from which I have made the following extracts. One omission regarding the Mission work I wish to supply, by pointing out the benefit that has accrued not only to the Mission, but also to Government, by Dr. Steere's labours in the native languages of Africa. The results are, in my opinion, so important that I consider they would alone amply repay the trouble and expense incurred by the Mission. Dr. Steere has established a small printing-press at Kangani, having already published in London the following books:—

"Steere's Swahili Tales." Bell and Daldy, 1870.
"Handbook of the Swahili Language." Ditto.

"Katekismo" (Swahili). Society for promoting Christian Knowledge.
"Scriptural Reading Lessons" (Swahili). Ditto.
"Psalms of David" (Swahili). Ditto.
"Collections for the Yao Language." Ditto.
"Collections for the Shambala Language." Ditto.
"Collections for the Nyamwesi Language." Ditto.

In addition to these works, Dr. Steere has in preparation and is printing at Kangani elementary books for instruction in arithmetic, reading, &c., chiefly in Swahili. These works cannot fail to be of great use to his fellow-missionaries, and to all foreigners on the coast.

2. The only other point in connection with the following extracts, on which I think it necessary to remark, is with regard to the salubrity of Zanzibar. I cannot but think that Dr. Steere takes too unfavourable a view of the effects of the climate: Zanzibar and the East Coast of Africa appear to me to be unhealthy from the same causes, and apparently not in much greater degree, than the West Coast of India; and the precautions taken in the latter place for the preservation of health would probably be equally efficacious if strictly observed in Zanzibar and East Africa. Caution against unnecessary exposure either to the sun or malaria, care with regard to drinking-water and food, and other obvious sanitary precautions, would probably go as far to lower the rate of mortality in Africa as they have done during the memory of living men in India.

Extracts from a Memorandum on the Present State and Prospects of the Central African Mission. By the Rev. E. Steere, D.C.L., &c. &c.

"As the Universities' Mission seems to have arrived at a crisis in its history, it is desirable that a clear account of its present position should be laid before those interested in its work; such an account I have, therefore, endeavoured to draw up. We are actually at work in three distinct places:—

"1. At Magila, among the heathen.

"2. In Zanzibar itself we have a girls' school, a vernacular service with an exposition of the Gospel every Sunday afternoon, daily prayers in Swahili and in English, and a weekly evening service with sermon, and Holy Communion twice in the month for the European residents.

"3. At Kingani, close to Zanzibar, we have our boys' school, and college for mission students. There are, of course, regular services in the chapel in English and in the vernacular. We have a printing-press at work, from which we have just issued, as the first of our school series, a Swahili spelling-book. An elementary arithmetic and a first reading-book are now in the press; we have also just begun to print Mr. Pennell's version of St. Luke's Gospel. Some hymns, a first catechism, and the Litany in Swahili have been printed since my arrival in Zanzibar in March 1872. Some of the boys work a saw-pit, and help in carpentering; the rest are engaged in bringing the land into order and cultivation.

"The special subjects on which our friends will look to us for information are, probably, the nature and prospect of our directly Mission-work, the results and present state of our school-work, the share we can take in the crusade against slavery, and the propriety of remaining at Zanzibar in spite of our many losses.

"I have tried to deal with these several matters as briefly and clearly as possible, and have subjoined an account of the property belonging to the Mission, with a list of its working members. Upon the data thus furnished, our friends at home will, I hope, be able to form a tolerably good judgment as to the results of past work, and the best form in which to proceed for the future.

"*Mission-work on the Mainland.*—A station has been established at a place called Magila, one long day's journey from the coast. It is now occupied by Samuel Speare, missionary student and sub-deacon, and Francis Mabruki, native sub-deacon.

"This site was selected chiefly with a view to health and convenience. There is much talk in England about 'healthy highlands,' but, so far as we can learn, there are none such. The truth seems to be that the fresh, cool air of any elevated region has, for a time, a very invigorating effect; and therefore every one who stays only for a few days or weeks, feels that the situation must be a healthy one. Such an opinion, however, is not confirmed by longer experience. It will be found that the spots described as unhealthy are chiefly those where some European has made a prolonged stay, and those described as healthy are those which have been visited for a short time only. There are, however, manifest advantages in an elevated location in such a climate as this; and as our experience on the Morumbala showed that a mountain swept by winds that had passed over a large swampy district was not exempt from the usual marsh fevers, we looked out for high land as near the coast as possible, in order to avoid the miasma. The most promising in every way seemed to be the mountain district known as Usambara. The mountains there come nearer to the coast than in any other place within the scope of our Mission, and they are so near as to be, in very clear weather, visible from the town of Zanzibar. Besides this, Dr. Krapf had always pointed to the Shambala country (Usambara) as peculiarly eligible as a mission field; and we had the good fortune to make the acquaintance of a singularly sensible and intelligent man, named Munyi Hatibu, who lives at Mworongo, the landing-place where the route into the Shambala country leaves the coast. All these considerations determined Bishop Tozer to attempt a first mainland station among these mountains. A vocabulary of the Shambala language was collected, and, as soon as circumstances permitted, the Rev. C. A. Allington was sent up, with two native boys as interpreters and attendants, to choose a site.

"After long delays and much unsatisfactory negotiation, the king of the country sent him to Magila, as the best or only place within his dominions where he would at that time allow him to build or to make any settlement.

"Mr. Allington was shortly after called back to England by a summons that could not be resisted, and then the charge of the Shambala Mission was given to the Rev. L. Fraser. Mr. Fraser preached in the villages within his reach, and instructed the children who were willing to be taught. His holy life and conversation had a great effect upon the natives with whom he came in contact, and his lessons are well remembered. He was hoping soon to have had some natives prepared for baptism, when he was called away during the frightful prevalence of cholera in this part of Eastern Africa. He was to have been succeeded by the Rev. O. Hancock, after whose sudden and premature death Magila remained unoccupied (except that it was visited twice by Bishop Tozer) until October 1872, when the two sub-deacons were sent up with instructions to occupy the post, and carry on such work as they could, until a clergyman could be found to superintend it. Their last letters spoke of themselves as settling down, and making arrangements for commencing a school, and some kind of public catechising or preaching.

"The Mission has an iron house and two large thatched native huts; the sub-deacons proposed to set up another as a school and temporary church.

"The prospects of this Mission cannot be well understood without a short account of the country and its government.

"The coast is occupied by the Swahili—a mixed race of Arabs and Negroes. They hold only the villages or small towns on the sea, and the gardens and plantations adjoining. The Swahili are all Mahomedans, chiefly of the Shafi sect. Behind their plantations lies a strip of country covered with long grass, and very scantily supplied with water. It is partly occupied by a Negro tribe, the Wadigo, who have their chief settlements to the northward. Where the hills begin to show themselves distinctly lie the villages of the half Swahili people, called by the coast men Washenzi, i.e. wild folk, and by the people of the mountains Waboonde, i.e. valley people. They talk a dialect of Swahili much mixed with Shambala words and phrases. The mountains themselves are occupied by the Shambala; but there is at least one large valley running up among them, which is occupied by the Zegulas, who are their next neighbours to the southward.

"Mr. Allington was very much disappointed at being sent back from Vuga, the chief town of the Shambala, to a place so near the coast as Magila. The reasons which swayed the native counsels seem to have been partly superstitious and partly political. The Shambala are a very shy and separate race. No foreigner was allowed to enter their chief town, and every means was ordinarily used to keep them at a distance; it happened besides, at this particular time, that no place in their own country would have been really a safe one.

"In Dr. Krapf's time they were ruled by an old king, named Kimweri, who had a very extensive influence. On his death great confusion followed. The mountain people chose a grandson of his, who took the name Kimweri and was in possession of Vuga at the time of Mr. Allington's visit. The lower country behind the mountains, that is, to the westward, was held by a son of old Kimweri's, named Semboja, and there was constant war between the two claimants. Before Mr. Allington left the country, young Kimweri died of small-pox, and was succeeded by a brother named Chenyegera. The war became more and more embittered, and Semboja, finding that the Shambalas would not receive him, encouraged all the neighbouring tribes to prey upon them. Chenyegera and his great men, finding themselves without money or arms, began selling their own people to the coast Arabs as slaves. Vuga was taken by Semboja and burnt, and a great part of the mountain country was depopulated and relapsed into forest land. At last the people rose upon their chiefs, and killed most of them, and so a peace of exhaustion has come at last. Semboja is in possession of most of the country, and is rebuilding Vuga. He is a Mahomedan, and has been supposed throughout to have had the silent support of the Zanzibar Arabs. Chenyegera is among the mountains, not very far from Magila. This last place itself has not been touched by the war, being geographically and politically in the Shambala country, but in language belonging to the valley people. These last have lately been at war with the Dagos, so that just now the coast Swahili are carrying on all the trade with Magila, the valley people being afraid to venture through the country of their enemies. There is now no actual fighting, and probably there will be no more for some time to come, as all parties are thoroughly worn out. The Shambala wars are said to have increased the population near Magila, many of the mountain people having come coastwards for safety.

"The station at Magila may be viewed as the first station among the Shambala, or as a starting-point for missions among them, and an actual occupation of the Boonde or low country; any station nearer the coast would be surrounded by Mahomedans. Through the Shambala country lies the road to the Wateila, Wassara, Wachaga, and other tribes about Kilmanjaro, the great snowy mountain.

"It may be worth consideration whether anything could be attempted among the Dagos. The next tribe to the northward are the Nyikas, where the Church Missionary Society has long been at work, and the United Free Methodists have also a station. In my own judgment we should do better to attempt the tribes to the southward.

"South of the Shambala lie the Zegulas, a very warlike and very barbarous tribe; next to them the Zaramos, through whose country lies the direct road to Ujiji and the great lakes. The chief tribe in this direction are the Myamwezi, though many smaller ones lie on the road to them. A Myamwezi vocabulary has been collected, in case it should be determined to make a bold plunge towards the central tribes. At present, however, a war of very uncertain result is going on between the native Myamwezi and the Arab and Swahili settlers in their country, and nothing could be reasonably attempted until that war has been concluded. Indeed the road to Ujiji is practically closed to any but special expeditions.

"South of the Zaramos lie the Gindos or Gendwas, and below them the Portuguese coast begins. Among the Gindos, not far from Lindy, between Kilwa and the Rovuma, a body of Yaos have settled, and are giving the coast people much trouble by receiving runaway slaves, and occasionally plundering the coast traders. Behind the Gindos, between them and the Lake Nyassa, lie the Yaos, and beyond it the Nyassas and the Bisas. I mention only the most important tribes, and that by their usual names. The Yaos are the Achawa of our earliest reports, and the Mang'aiya were Nyassas.

"It is in this direction that our work ought most naturally to develop itself, and Bishop Tozer has always contemplated a journey to the Lake Nyassa. The great hindrance has been the devastation of the country by the Maviti, probably the Mazitu of Dr. Livingstone's earlier books. They have swept the country up to Kilwa, plundering and murdering everywhere. Their chief seats are said now to be on the Rovuma, they having suffered severe losses in their attacks upon some of the most powerful Yao chieftains. A great stretch of country on the road to the Nyassa is now a wilderness.

"As a starting-point on the road to the lakes, the caravans usually cross to Bagamoyo for Ujiji, and go down to Kilwa for the Nyassa. Bagamoyo is occupied by an extensive settlement under the care of a French Roman Catholic mission, which has also houses in Zanzibar itself. At a short distance to the south lies Dar-es-Salaam, which the Sultan of Zanzibar's predecessor intended to make the starting-point for all caravans going into or coming from any part of the interior. From Dar-es-Salaam to Kilwa the coast is little known, and is reputed to be very unhealthy. South of Kilwa there are many good harbours; the coast is often hilly, and there are many convenient landing-places. I have always myself thought of Lindy as one that might well be chosen. The further south one goes, the shorter the land journey to the Lake Nyassa becomes. In contemplation of mission-work in this direction, we have collected a vocabulary of the Yao language, and hope some day to be allowed to use the very complete dictionary of the Nyassa language compiled by the Rev. John Rebmann of Kissoludini, near Mombassa, which now only exists in a jealously-guarded MS.

"I do not see any reason why stations should not at once be planted among the Zegulas, the Zaramos, and the Gindos near the coast, or among the Yaos and Nyassas near Lake Nyassa, or among some of the tribes on the road to Ujiji. I feel sure that missionaries would be safe anywhere, and all the more so if they were known to carry no arms whatever: Negroes are very seldom violent unless they are frightened, and, besides, there is nothing so tempting to a native thief as European fire-arms. It was a well-grounded boast of Dr. Krapf that he went with only an umbrella where others dare not venture fully armed. I believe myself that arms are a cause of insecurity, and can never be of any use to a missionary. (The idea of founding a settlement by force ought not to be entertained for a moment. One may fight one's way through a country, but one can never hold it by violence; besides that, the secular business of a fighting chief would soon swallow up his missionary character. A king must tolerate many things which a bishop is bound to denounce.)

"*The Slave Trade and Released Slaves.*—The complete suppression of the Slave Trade and slavery can only come about by the Christianization of the Africans themselves. The coast Slave Trade is by no means the only one existing; slavery is found everywhere; and its mild character in the interior arises only from the same cause which makes Arab slavery lighter than slavery to Europeans, and that is the smaller difference, morally and socially, between the slave and his master.

"Slavery may be attacked politically or religiously—politically we may attack it by treaties with native powers, enforced by armed intervention; religiously it can only be attacked by self-sacrifice, and by acting upon the minds of those who uphold it. The two methods require very different men to carry them forward, and cannot both be attempted by the same persons with any reasonable chance of success.

"The way in which slavery was actually destroyed in

Christendom was by elevating the slave while still a slave. Christian slaves were such extraordinary good slaves that the masters and mistresses began to see a divine power working in them. It is to such a result that St. Paul points continually, and such results did actually follow; meanwhile, Christian masters became ashamed to use the powers which they by law possessed. A suppression of slavery brought about in this way must be final.

"Leaving, therefore, to our political leaders the task of external repression, it belongs to us missionaries to aim at the internal work. As things actually are in Eastern Africa, our first thought will naturally be given to the released slaves, set free by English cruisers. It seems politicians consider that their work is done when the gift of political freedom is complete; we know that very much more is needed.

"It is sometimes assumed that to put released slaves under the superintendence of Englishmen or Scotchmen is all that is needed. I wish it were so; but a little experience shows that, just as a European can be much better than a Negro, so he can be much worse, and that when possessed of absolute power, and free from the control of home opinion, he probably will use the Negro only to serve his own selfish ends and cast him off as soon as he has served them. Neither by example, nor in any other way, are such Europeans as ordinarily settle in remote places likely to do any great amount of good to the Negro.

"Politically, the protection of the English name may save a released man in Eastern Africa from being forcibly re-inslaved; but, in order to do him much good, he must have a means of livelihood opened to him, and must be brought at least within hearing of Christian teaching.

"So much has been said already on this subject, that one need only point out, as the duty of this Mission, to be ready to give all such help as the men and money at its command may allow to any and every scheme for the benefit of the slaves and released slaves within the district in which it works. It must not be forgotten, however, that missions in the interior are, after all, the chief means by which the regeneration of the Negro must be accomplished.

"We have taken in as many boys and girls as our funds allowed, and Bishop Tozer bought some land, with a view to planting out on it grown-up persons; whether more is to be done in this direction must depend upon our subscribers at home. I think myself that in our poverty the feeding and lodging of any except very promising children, who are likely to become missionaries or teachers, are not proper charges on the Mission funds.

"*Mission Schools and College.*—The schools at Zanzibar were formed by Bishop Tozer for the purpose of educating missionaries and teachers, and their future wives, for work among the inland tribes. The scholars are now beginning to attain an age at which they may be actively employed. Three of the boys have been set apart as sub-deacons; of these, one was lost by the cholera, the other two are both married—one, John Swedi, is at present acting as a sort of assistant-chaplain at the school at Kingani; the other, Francis Mabruki, is working at the Shambala Mission station at Magila.

"It was always hoped and intended that these schools should be filled by the children of converts, or by promising young people from the Mission stations among the inland tribes. The only scholars we have yet had answering this description were three Nyika lads from the Rev. John Robinson's station near Mombassa. They stayed with us about two years, and then returned to their friends. For the rest we have been obliged to depend upon the captures made by English cruisers and seizures made by the Sultan of Zanzibar. There is, of course, always a question how far children so chosen may turn out to have any fitness for missionary work.

"The future of the schools must depend upon the sources from which they are to be supplied with scholars. If we have the choice of promising boys and girls from our Mission stations, we may hope to be able to lead them on to a much higher style of training than has been as yet possible. If, on the other hand, they are to be filled from the slave-dhows, it will be necessary to introduce a much larger industrial element. In any case, we hope to give all alike, first, a plain education in Swahili, for which the necessary books are in course of preparation, and then to give the best scholars a thorough grounding in English. We are anxious to increase the number of girls, as otherwise our lads, especially the duller ones, who will have to get their living by daily work. will be sorely tempted to turn Muhammedans as the only means of obtaining wives.

"After the work, which one regards as merely school-work, is completed, there will remain something of college-work, intended exclusively for our future missionaries. It was with a view to this that the house at Kingani was begun, and the proceeds of the Wells Tozer Fund, and the grant made by the Society for the Promotion of Christian Knowledge, were applied towards the cost of its buildings. It was intended here to join with the native students others from England, who might thus be enabled to make themselves acquainted with the language and manners of the East Africans while still pursuing their general studies. Two students have already joined us, and, under Mr. Pennell's care, were making good progress. It has become necessary for a time to employ them elsewhere, but their studies are not wholly interrupted, while the great object of becoming familiar with the details of Mission-work in East Africa is only being the more completely carried out. This college-work is one of very great importance, and it ought not to be difficult to secure efficient help in it, as any clergyman who could leave England for a few years could undertake it, all the scholars being either English or English-speaking natives. We have had an earnest hope that some of the young incumbents of small rural parishes, who feel that they are in danger of getting rusty for want of real work, might be willing to leave their charges for a time in the hands of well-chosen curates and come to our assistance, and that the heads of the Church would encourage them in so laudable an undertaking. The Bishops have power to grant licences for absence on such works as these, and it is surely better that an active young man should be so employed than that he should be held strictly to such pastoral work only as a cure of two or one hundred, or even fewer, souls may supply him, under the penalty of giving up all hope of a home for his more advanced age.

"To be obliged to give up all prospects elsewhere in order to help in such a Mission as ours is a greater sacrifice than it is quite reasonable to expect any great number of English clergymen to make, although as Christ's soldiers they ought not to be unwilling to adventure it. Even those trained in missionary colleges are likely to prefer healthier and better known spheres. It becomes, therefore, a very necessary thing to give men an opportunity of testing their health and their fitness for the work without robbing them of valuable time. This our Mission pupil scheme specially provides for, by occupying, in mingled study and work at Zanzibar, the years between sixteen and twenty, which a young man with a mission vocation finds it so difficult in England to employ to any advantage. While the missionaries of the future are thus growing up, we must have temporary help from special English sources. There are hundreds who could give it us without any real danger to themselves.

"*Zanzibar and its Unhealthiness.*—There is no act to which the credit of Bishop Tozer and his advisers is more distinctly pledged than to the choice of Zanzibar as the point of departure of the Central African Mission. He was severely censured for this choice, in words, by Dr. Livingstone, but was absolved by that great traveller, in deeds, when he himself chose Zanzibar as his starting-point whence to revisit the River Shire and the Lake Nyassa. The matter is not one on which missionaries have any real choice. The centre of any considerable missionary operations must be the centre fixed beforehand by the many circumstances which together have determined the position of the chief city; missionaries must travel along the usual road, and their lines of communication can only be those created by commercial intercourse.

"The great objection made to Zanzibar is the unhealthiness, shown by so many deaths among the members of the Mission.

This is a very startling consideration, and one naturally asks oneself, How can so unhealthy a place be so great a centre of commerce, and how can it be that European merchants consent to live there as they undoubtedly do? The answer is a remarkable one; it is that the great mortality is confined to the members of the Mission. There have been a much larger number of other Europeans residing in the town, and the Mission has lost five members, while they have lost only two or three. Ill-health is common, but death is very rare. One Frenchman, who had been settled here more than twenty years, died lately; but, except this, the deaths have all been among British subjects. In fact, no German, American, or French merchant has died within memory, and yet the merchants are more exposed to the sun than we are, and are less temperate livers. The only obvious difference between the Mission and the mercantile houses is, that the merchants seldom remain more than three years in Zanzibar without a change; only one of those missionaries, however, who have died had lived in Zanzibar nearly as much as three years. It seems to follow that there must have been special causes at work, and it remains to discover and to prevent them."

[Dr. Steere then enters into details, showing that, of the missionaries who had died, one was suffering from a fatal disease of long standing; one died from cholera, which was everywhere fatal; two from over-fatigue and exposure during a journey into the interior of the mainland; and two from dysentery: other ailments always having given way to change of climate. "My own impression after very careful observation and inquiry from all best informed on the subject is that Zanzibar and the East African coast may compare favourably with any part of the Indian coast as regards natural salubrity. There are many causes of insalubrity which used to affect the resident on the Indian coast, but which now affect him no longer, owing to better knowledge of localities and more and better appliances to resist the effects of climate. I have no doubt that in time the same will be found to be the case in Africa.—H. B. E. F.]

"It seems then to follow, not that Zanzibar should be abandoned as hopelessly unhealthy, but that very special care should be taken to avoid any known danger to health, and that frequent leave of absence should be given. It is possible that the proposed line of mail-steamers between Natal and Zanzibar may furnish the means of securing a change of climate without entirely quitting the missionary field; and Bishop Wilkinson, before leaving England, actually discussed with me the possibility of an occasional exchange of labourers between the two Missions. It must, however, be remembered that the permanence of any regular communication between Zanzibar and the Cape is very uncertain.*

"The existence of any really healthy site on the mainland of Africa is exceedingly doubtful. Healthy highlands in the interior are often spoken of, as though their position were well known; but this is only because the geography of this part of Africa is very little understood. The centre of the continent is, as we now know, nothing but a large swamp. From the coast the land rises very gently to the watershed, and then drops very gradually to the great swampy central basin. Groups and ridges of mountains are scattered about, without any distinct connection with the general rise of the land. There is nothing analogous to the terraces described as existing in Natal, nor is there any particular district of which it can be said that it is high and healthy. These facts were the ground upon which Bishop Tozer based his great plan for training native missionaries.

"There is no use in dissembling the fact that Eastern Africa is exceedingly unhealthy, and that not on the coast only, but in every part."

[I very much doubt this being the case as a permanent fact. The same might have been said of India till we found out how to live there and preserve health. I am sure that no men could live in India as I saw some of my countrymen living in Zanzibar, with such disregard of exposure and neglect of sanitary precautions without losing health, and often, life.—H. B. E. F.]

* A permanent line of mail steamers, running once a month from Aden to the Cape, has been established since Dr. Steere wrote.

"It is only now and then that a man can be found with a constitution so well adapted to the climate that he can live safely in it for more than a few years at a time. Even in the case of those who are not attacked by any distinct disease, languor and incapacity for mental exertion are sure after a while to show themselves. It follows clearly that a white missionary's proper work must be to train and to superintend native preachers. They must be the permanent missionaries and the regular pastors of the negro church. So long as it is expected of our missionaries that they will stay, say ten years at least, in some particular district, so long it is very possible that the terrible mortality we all deplore may continue. We must arrange for frequent changes, and that place will be best fitted for our centre of operations in which good medical advice, good lodgings, and the comforts that are needed in sickness are most easily obtained, and, above all, from which it will be possible for the head of the Mission to send away in time those who will surely die if they stay in Africa, and will surely live if they can get to a more temperate region. These advantages are nowhere to be found so certainly as at Zanzibar. There is nothing we should be more glad to find than a healthy location, and even a comparatively healthy spot would be at once occupied.

"In any case, however, so long as Zanzibar remains what it is, the Mission must have a home there of some kind. It is very probable that if (as has been often proposed) the British Government should establish a colony of freed men near some convenient port, the town, which would soon grow up, might supplant Zanzibar as a commercial centre, in which case the Mission would, as of course, remove thither its head-quarters.

"*Mission Property.*—The Mission property consists of land and houses for the use of its members. We have—

"1. In Zanzibar itself, a large house in the part of the town called Shangani, used as a girls' school, and a portion capable of separate occupation as lodgings for the Bishop. The house is close to the sea, and a very fine one, the rooms being large and very lofty. It was procured cheaply, owing to its having been abandoned by the natives from fear of a spirit which was supposed to haunt it. Not having been occupied for some time, it was in need of much repair, and many alterations were necessary to adapt what might be described as an Arab palace to our purposes. Although so very large, we found only six rooms available for use. It was at one time proposed to purchase this house for the English Political Residency;* it may be worth consideration whether, if a good price is offered, it might not be well to accept it, and to find or build a more convenient school-house for girls elsewhere. The question as to where the Bishop will for the future fix his general residence is, of course, most important in this respect. Extensive repairs were rendered necessary by the cyclone, and are still in progress.

"2. A very small house, a short distance behind the larger one. It has been used as a lodging for guests and others for whom there was no room elsewhere, and, when necessary, as a small-pox hospital.

"3. A piece of land (perhaps about eight acres) about two miles out of the town known as Kingani, or among the natives as Kinma Mgnu, on which stand the buildings occupied as a boys' school, and sometimes called St. Andrew's College. It is admirably situated for health, but the soil is very barren. Extensive repairs are going on here also.

"4. A small piece of land (perhaps about two acres) containing the mud-and-thatch house occupied by the subdeacon, John Swedi, who cultivates a portion of it. It is near, but not adjoining, to the larger Kingani premises.

"5. A piece of fertile land (about thirteen acres) nearly five miles from the town, with a small stone house upon it, known as Mbweni. The house is in very bad repair, and the value of the property was almost entirely destroyed by the cyclone. Out of 600 cocoa-nut trees only 19 were left standing.

* This, I believe, has since been done, and on Christmas Day, 1873, the first stone of "Christ Church" was laid by Capt. Prideaux, the officiating Consul-General, and Dr. Steere, on the site of the old Slave Market in the town of Zanzibar.

"6. At Magila, an iron house and some native buildings. The land was occupied under a special authority from the then king, which is almost the only right in land capable of being acquired among the Shambalas.

"7. At Mworongo, the landing-place for Magila, we have helped Munji Hatibu to build an upper room to his house, on condition that we have the use of it on our journey to and fro.

"*Mission Staff in Zanzibar, December* 1872.—1, Rev. E. Steere; 2, Mr. Moreton, General Superintendent at Kingani; 3, Samuel Speare and Benjamin Hartley, missionary pupils; 4, John Swedi and Francis Mabruki, native sub-deacons.

"NOTE.

"1. The total number of Negroes who have come under the care of the Universities' Mission since its settlement at Zanzibar is 110, all of whom were received as children. There are now 48 males and 24 females under the immediate care of the Mission. Of these, two males and two females are now adults. There are besides two of the former scholars employed as sub-deacons by the Mission, and four males who have lately left the mission-house to go into service in the town.

"2. Of the Negroes now actually under the care of the Mission, 44 males and 23 females were received from Her Majesty's Government.

"3. The children under the care of the Mission are instructed in English and Swahili, with a view to their employment in connection with the mainland stations of the Mission. The elder children act as pupil-teachers: some of the boys (at present six of them) are engaged in the printing-office, others have been taught carpentering: the girls are taught needlework—and all, both boys and girls, take their share in cooking, cleaning the house, and waiting at table, besides keeping the grounds in order, and assisting in any special work that may occur.

(Signed) "EDWARD STEERE,
Priest in charge to the Mission."

I now resume my quotations from the Parliamentary Blue Book.

II. FRENCH MISSION.

"The French Mission has been established for several years at Zanzibar, where they have extensive mission premises in the town, and a small plantation two or three miles off. In the town, besides the accommodation required for the Brethren and their pupils, the chapel, &c., they have a forge and smith's workshop, where a great deal of engine-work is turned out by the pupils. Besides attending school, where they get a good elementary education in French, they have learned to form a military band, and some of them prove very apt musical scholars.

"The Brethren used to have a hospital, where they gave gratuitous attendance and medicine. The institution was a great blessing to the town and to the shipping in harbour; but since the French Government have been compelled to withdraw the services of the surgeon who was formerly allowed to the institution, the Brethren have been obliged to close their hospital to all but special cases of Europeans, who are still received and tended by the Brethren as far as their means and skill allow.

"But their principal station is at the establishment of Notre Dame de Bagamoyo, near the mouth of the Kingani, on the mainland opposite Zanzibar, to the detailed account of which, as given below, I would request special attention.

"Here have been established, for about four and a half years, four Sisters of Charity from a convent at Réunion, and five Brethren under two Fathers of the order of St. Esprit et du St. Cœur de Marie, the head-quarters of which are at No. 30, Rue Lhomond, in Paris. They train about 15 adult liberated Africans, and about 150 boys and 100 girls, for the most part liberated slaves captured by British cruisers. They have about eighty acres of land reclaimed from the African forest and in cultivation, and had built wholesome and sufficient buildings, including a chapel and a library, separate huts for sick and visitors, &c., when the hurricane of last year destroyed the whole, with the exception of one hut; and though, providentially, no life was lost, the whole place was for the time utterly ruined. The Brethren are now, as far as their means will permit, rebuilding everything in a more permanent style. They have never intermitted the hospitality with which they treat all strangers and travellers, and which we enjoyed during the very pleasant days we spent at their Mission.

"I can suggest no change in the general arrangements of the institution, with any view to increase its efficiency as an industrial and civilising agency, and in that point of view I would recommend it as a model to be followed in any attempt to civilise or evangelise Africa. All that can be desired in its secular arrangements—and of them alone I am now speaking—is an extension of the means which have been so well applied by Père Horner and his reverend colleagues. There is little room for expansion where they are now, but a branch establishment may be formed at a little distance in the interior, which would materially aid all the objects of the parent institution.

"Possibly the Fathers may be able to obtain for themselves all they require for the formation of such a branch establishment, or for any additions they may require to the land they now hold near Bagamoyo. But should they require and wish for assistance, I think it should be afforded to them by the British Consul in the same way as I have proposed for the Universities' Mission, without reference to the nationality of an institution so judiciously promoting the objects which the British Government has in view for the freedom and civilisation of East Africa.

"I gathered from the reverend Fathers that there was practically no limit to the number of children they could accommodate, if they were added gradually, so as to admit of their labour aiding in the expense of their maintenance, or if payments were made for such as could earn nothing for their own support."

The following information regarding the Mission was kindly furnished to me by Père Horner:—

(Translation.)

"M. LE MINISTRE,   *Notre Dame de Bagamoyo, Feb. 3, 1873.*

"I have the honour to inclose herewith detailed replies

to the questions which your Excellency was pleased to address to me, on behalf of your Government, on the subject of our Mission and its labours.

"To avoid misunderstanding I wish to give a short explanation. Our establishment is not at present in its usual state. In consequence of the cruel hardships and many difficulties we had to undergo after the destruction of our dwellings by the hurricane of the 15th April last, several members of the Mission died or were invalided home to Europe.

"In all probability five 'religieuses' are now on their way to reinforce the establishment of sisters; priests and brethren are expected shortly. I shall, therefore, count our numbers in their usual force, and as we soon shall be.

"Accept, &c.
(Signed) "HORNER."

(Translation.)

"*Answers to Questions put to the Rev. Père Horner, Superior of the Zanzibar French Mission, by Sir H. B. E. Frere.*

"1st. The Society to which the Catholic Mission of Zanzibar belongs is called the 'Société du Saint Esprit et du Saint Cœur de Marie;' its head-quarters are at Paris, Rue Lhomond (ancienne rue des Postes). This society supplies fathers and brothers to the said Mission.

"The 'Superior-General' of this society is 'Préfet Apostolique' of Zanzibar; but he has delegated all his powers to Père Horner, whom he has named 'Vice-Préfet Apostolique.'

"The Rev. Père Horner is also Vice-Provincial 'Supérieur' of the ecclesiastics employed on the Mission.

"He thus combines a double authority, viz. ecclesiastic and religious.

"The Sisters, to whom the education of the girls at the Mission is intrusted, belong to the Society of the 'Filles de Marie,' whose head-quarters are at St. Denis in Réunion.

"All the Sisters are subordinate to Père Horner, and are superintended by a 'Supérieure Provinciale.'

"2nd. The governing body at the Mission is composed as follows:—

"(1.) The community of St. Joseph of Zanzibar, possessing two priests and four brothers, with one lay professor of music.

"(2.) The community of Notre Dame de Bagamoyo, comprising four priests, eight brothers, and twelve sisters, with two lay brothers employed in agriculture.

"3rd. There are at present under the Zanzibar Mission 324 Negroes. Of these 324 persons, 73 are adults and 251 are children.

"4th. We have received 172 freed slaves from the British Government.

"5th. The occupations of the various classes are divided as follows:—

"(1.) Children. Primary schools.

"Including religious instruction. Children pass five and a-half hours a day in the primary school, and the same length of time at manual labour.

"(2.) Arts and trades.

"Children who are employed in the workshops, and are learning different trades, only spend one hour in the primary school, and receive half an hour's religious instruction daily.

"(3.) Agricultural section.

"This is composed of children who show no aptitude for study. With the exception of half an hour devoted to religious instruction and an hour of the most elementary lessons, all their time, viz. nine hours daily, is spent in agricultural pursuits.

"*Girls.*—1st. Primary school.

"Very young girls follow the same course as the corresponding class of boys, except that some of their time is spent in sewing.

"2nd. Working section.

"Girls who have no aptitude for study only spend one hour a day in elementary lessons, and half an hour in receiving religious instruction. Five hours during the day are devoted to working in the fields, and the rest in learning sewing and other household duties.

"6th. There is a small seminary of nineteen pupils under the Mission at Zanzibar for the education of a native clergy.

"Amongst this number there are hopes of finding future Brothers and Catechists to regenerate the country.

"There is also at Bagamoyo a noviciate of five girls who wish to become native Sisters.

"These two bodies are drawn from our primary schools."

     (Signed)   "HORNER.

"*Notre Dame de Bagamoyo, February* 3, 1873."

(Translation.)

"M. LE MINISTRE,

"In accordance with the wishes of your Excellency, I have the honour to forward you a brief memorandum relative to the disposition of slaves liberated by the English Government.

"Your Excellency can well understand that merely to liberate the Negroes, without according them the succour of Christian civilisation, would be quite insufficient to insure their happiness, or to make them useful members of society. You are come to give the blessings of liberty to the wretched slaves, and we shall be happy to give you our utmost help in so praiseworthy a mission.

"Nobody can ignore the fact that the natural apathy and indolence peculiar to the negro character form the greatest obstacles to his 'moralisation;' and it is only by degrees that we can conquer their vices, by inspiring them with a regard and love of work according to the principles of Christianity.

"But it must be acknowledged that this system of education requires material, no less than personal, sacrifices.

"Permit me then to explain to you in detail the conditions of the various classes of liberated negroes who might, at any time, be confided to our care.

"These liberated slaves can be divided into three distinct categories from this point of view:—

"1st. Healthy men, able to work.

"2nd. Old men and women, and infirm people.

"3rd. Infants of tender age, who are not able to earn their own living by work.

"*First.*—Healthy men, able to work.

"I have no hesitation in saying that a negro in good health, and of a working age, can earn his own living. But it is easy to understand that the newly-arrived liberated slaves are but little accustomed to work.

"Consequently it is necessary at the commencement to 'coax' them ('les ménager') to prevent their running away, and to allow them a great latitude until such time as they may be accustomed to work.

"During this time these men consume much but produce nothing. Moreover, as on their arrival they possess nothing at all, it is necessary to furnish them with a lodging, with clothing, with the most indispensable household utensils, and also with tools for work.

"Still more, it is necessary to procure for them a happiness greater than that of the past, to render their life more agreeable, to attach them to their work, and to prevent them from returning to their primitive state of barbarism.

"To obtain these results, I consider indispensable a sum of 125 fr. per man, to liquidate the cost of his first equipment and subsequent entertainment. This sum would only be required once, on the first arrival of the negro.

"*Second.*—Old and infirm people.

"It occasionally happens, though rarely, that there are found, among the liberated slaves, some aged people so 'overwhelmed' ('accablés') with infirmities that they are quite incapable of work.

"This class of slaves demands the largest pecuniary sacrifices, for the following reasons:—

"Firstly, in addition to the necessity of providing them with the equipment mentioned in the preceding paragraph, it will also be needful to support these men until their death, without their being able to gain anything for their livelihood. Besides, as they are deprived of all support from their families, and have no one to administer the attentions so necessary in sickness and infirmity, they will require particular personal attendance to wait upon them. Again, these infirm people will require, in addition to medicines, a better description of food. Considering all these expenses, I think that this class of slaves should be estimated to cost at least 60 centimes per day per man.

"*Third.*—Children.

"In this class there are two descriptions of children:—

"(1.) Children of the age of twelve years and under, who are incapable of earning their living by work.

"(2.) Children from twelve to fifteen years, who can contribute something by work to the cost of their subsistence.

"The first class would be entirely supported by the establishment.

"Taking into consideration the cost of construction, of the material for schools, and for the support of the institutors, I do not think a sum of 50 centimes per child per day would be too much. With regard to those children who could already contribute something to their subsistence, I think 25 centimes per child per day to be reasonable.

"Such are the cases in which I shall be happy to co-operate with your Excellency in aiding your general plans.

"Yet, as the increase of the Negroes would naturally necessitate that of the superintendents, I could come to no definite arrangement till I had consulted with the Very Reverend Father Superior, head of the 'Congrégation du Saint Esprit et du Saint Cœur de Marie,' under whom I am, and who provides the missionaries for the work of civilisation ('moralisation') which I direct.

"Receive, &c.

(Signed) "HORNER."

(Translation.)

"M. LE MINISTRE,   *Zanzibar, January* 27, 1873.

"I have the honour to inform your Excellency that, during the last two years, Dr. Kirk has made over to this Mission about 200 freed slaves, who will thus enjoy the advantages of civilisation.

"Up till now we have done our utmost to meet his benevolent and enlightened views, and have been always grateful to him for his lively sympathy with our work.

"Till quite recently, by increased labour and sacrifices, we have been able to carry on our work without asking any support from the Government which he so well represents. Most gladly and willingly would I continue to do so; but, M. le Ministre, the hurricane of the 15th April, 1872, carried away almost all our buildings at Bagamoyo, and financially ruined the Mission. Some of the children sent us by Dr. Kirk are temporarily most wretchedly lodged, and suffer thereby both in health and morals. This makes me trust that your Excellency will look favourably on the confidence I place in you, in frankly explaining to you the great and urgent need of our Mission. I am fully convinced that the Government of Great Britain will come to our aid, and better the lot of the poor Negroes whom they have confided to our care. The state of our finances will cause the rebuilding of our establishment at Bagamoyo to be a slow and tedious operation. Consequently we shall, now and for some time to come, find great difficulty in providing shelter for any liberated slaves who may be sent to us.

"Your Excellency will, I feel sure, understand that real necessity dictates this appeal—an appeal which rests on the confidence I place in your Excellency, and on the generosity of that Government of which you are the noble and worthy representative.

"Accept, &c.

(Signed) "HORNER."

"*Remarks by Mr. Hill, Secretary to the Mission, on Memorandum by Père Horner, Superior of the Roman Catholic Mission at Zanzibar and Bagamoyo.*

"THE organisation of the French Roman Catholic Mission at Bagamoyo is so fully described in the preceding papers that very little remains to be said on that head, but some of Père Horner's opinions seem to call for a few remarks.

"The manner in which the Fathers carry out their theory, that the Negro should learn to be a useful member of society whilst he is being taught the doctrines of Christianity is so admirably practical as to leave nothing to desire to insure the success which attends their efforts. But when Père Horner insists on the inborn indolence and apathy of the Negro, does he not, perhaps, forget that most of those who come under his observation are unfortunate beings, in whom the sufferings they have undergone since they were carried off from their homes into slavery may have deadened all energy? And is this lack of energy to be wondered at, when we think that the idea ever present in their minds must be that the work they do brings them no gain, but only profit to a master who shares none of it with them, and who would sell them at once if it suited his pocket to do so? A very short time under the kind care of this Mission must, I am sure, suffice to disabuse them of this idea, and make them willing workers. We saw so many symptoms of a willingness to work when once they were sure that work meant prosperity to themselves, and not the labour of a slave for the good of his master, that I am convinced the liberated negro is indolent through ignorance more than through any idleness inborn in the East African race. For this reason I think that Père Horner has undervalued the labour of the adult Negroes on his Mission ground; and, in future, now that that ground is considerably developed and cultivated, the force of example will be stronger on new-comers than it has hitherto been.

"His theory of attracting them at first by comforts superior to those to which they have been accustomed, is indisputably correct in a place where there is no power of physical restraint.

"Père Horner says that, within the last two years, he has received from Dr. Kirk, in round numbers, 200 slaves set free by our ships, i.e. at the rate of 100 a-year; that of these, the adults are soon able to support themselves: boys and girls of over twelve years of age can contribute something to their own maintenance, while children and the aged or invalid are alone a direct burthen to the establishment. This burthen, he says, is especially trying at present, when the funds of the Mission are impoverished by the hurricane of 1872, which destroyed many of its buildings, as well as by the poverty caused in Alsace by the late war. He remarks on the increased sacrifices thus entailed on the Mission, and estimates the sum which, under the present conditions, he thinks necessary to support our liberated slaves, as follows:—

"For adults, a bonus of 5*l*.
"For aged and invalid, 6*d*. per day.
"For children under twelve, 5*d*. per day.
"For children over twelve, 2½*d*. per day.

"This seems rather a high estimate, for it is partly based on a presumed necessity for continual construction of buildings, and there can be no reason why this should be, if once a sum of money were found to erect houses sufficiently large to meet the probable requirements.

"If a subscription were set on foot amongst English Roman Catholics, this want would doubtless be soon met.

"It is difficult at present to judge what effect the enforcement of more rigorous anti-Slave Trade measures may have in increasing the number of slaves to be cared for; but with the numerous other means of disposal at our command, it is not likely that there will be many more than 100 per annum sent to the care of the Bagamoyo Mission, and, with the cessation of the Slave Trade, of course this number would correspondingly diminish. Moreover in considering the sacrifices which, as Père Horner justly points out, the missionaries are called upon to make on behalf of these liberated slaves, we must not forget the *raison d'être* of the Mission is the welfare of the African race, and in no way can a large number of Africans be better or more immediately aided than by the care which is bestowed on these sufferers.

"It is clear, however, that Great Britain, who has taken on herself the duty of liberating slaves, is bound, even at a large cost, to see that they are not the sufferers by her acts.

"There is at this moment no place in every way so suited to receive and properly educate them as the Bagamoyo Mission. Instead, however, of accepting Père Horner's plan of paying a daily sum for their subsistence, I would suggest that it would be more economical for us, and more advantageous to the Mission, now in immediate want of funds, that we should pay a bonus of 5*l.* for every freed slave, young or old, handed over to their care. This would find funds for providing the negro with proper clothing and tools, and, in the case of those over twelve years of age, would maintain them till they were able to earn their own subsistence.

"Objections may very likely be raised to thus encouraging a Roman Catholic institution; but till our missionary societies will follow their example and train up their pupils to be useful citizens as well as pious Christians, what is to be done? It is surely better that these pagan Africans should learn Christianity, even in a form with which we do not agree, than that they should be left in their present benighted state. What these Roman Catholic Fathers have done, our English missionaries could do as well; and an opportunity is now afforded at the Church Missionary Society's station at Kissoludini, near Mombassa, which, if properly taken advantage of and supported by Her Majesty's Government, would at once form a Protestant home for very many liberated slaves, and a starting-point of the greatest value to civilisation and to commerce.

     (Signed) "CLEMENT LL. HILL.

"*April* 12, 1873."*

---

* Since this was written, Père Horner has returned to France, and, by stating the wants of his Mission to the friends of his Church in some of the great seminaries and cities of France, has, I am informed, obtained all the aid he required, in men as well as in money.

III. CHURCH MISSIONARY SOCIETY'S MISSION.

"The Church Missionary Society has, for thirty years past, had a mission at Mombassa, with a branch establishment at Kissoludini close to Rabbai, about six miles from the head of a branch of the great estuary, the mouth of which forms the port of Mombassa. The Mission was begun in 1844 by Dr. Krapf, who had been for many years previously labouring in Abyssinia.

"When we visited these places, Mr. Rebmann was the only European missionary present. He probably ranks among the oldest and most learned missionaries now in Africa, and has laboured longer on the East Coast than any one now living there. He has specially devoted himself to the study of the native languages, and, besides some translations of the Scriptures, has completed three dictionaries of the Nyassa, the Kanika, and the Swahili tongues, two of which are absolutely ready for the printer, whilst the third only requires transcription.) His health has of late years quite failed him, and I much fear that, unless relieved, he may die at his post, and many of the invaluable collections, the results of so many years of literary toil, may be lost, as he is unwilling to part with them. He has been unable of late years to take much active part in more direct missionary work; and we found but eight converts at Kissoludini, and five of them belonged to two families which had joined from the African Orphanage at Nassick, near Bombay. Mr. Rebmann has insuperable scruples regarding the admission of anything like an industrial or worldly element into the teaching or action of the Mission, and his influence has consequently been limited to the example of a holy life of ascetic self-denial and indifference to all worldly enjoyments and employments, which have had the usual effect of exciting the admiration, without securing the imitation, of the people around him.

"I gathered, however, from the conversations I had with Mr. George David, a very intelligent catechist whom we found in charge at Kissoludini, that he had no doubt of the success of any extension of the Mission which should give to it more of an industrial element, similar to that in which he was himself trained at Nassick. The people around are willing enough to come and listen, and approve of the truths they hear; but if, when they ask what they shall do, the missionary declines to follow St. Paul's or St. John the Baptist's example, and simply exhorts them to believe, they are too often inclined to defer compliance to some more convenient season, and to conclude that Christianity is compatible with no worldly status but that of the ascetic or the salaried teacher of a foreign dogma.

"Mr. George David had no doubt that, if set to agriculture or other industrial occupations, numbers of the people round would flock to the Mission. It would be difficult to find a better situation for it, in every point of view; and I feel assured that, if placed under a superintendent who, like Mr. Price at Nassick, added to judicious missionary zeal great powers of organisation, results might be secured far surpassing what I have witnessed at Nassick, for there is a total absence of the old fossilised superstitious caste-prejudices and social difficulties which form so powerful an obstacle to the labours of the missionary in India.

"The buildings erected by Mr. Rebmann at Kissoludini are well-planned and substantial as far as they are completed, and the establishment is in every way capable of indefinite expansion."

IV. METHODIST MISSION.

"Much of what has been stated of Kissoludini is, to some extent, true of Ribe, the station of the United Methodist Free Churches, where Messrs. New and Wakefield have been labouring for the last ten or eleven years. Both gentlemen are distinguished for the great additions they have made to geographical knowledge during extended missionary tours to the snowy mountain, Kilimanjaro, and into the Galla country. We saw, at their ordinary Sunday-school assemblies and services, between forty and fifty converts and inquirers, many of them Gallas, members of broken tribes harassed by Masai and Somali inroads. They had sought refuge with the missionaries, whose acquaintance they had made during their tours, and they testified to a wide-spread impression that peace and good-will, so rare in their own country, were characteristics of the Christian settlement.

"Here, as at the neighbouring Mission, the most conspicuous defect seemed to me the want of a larger admixture of the industrial element—of more direct teaching how to live in this world, as well as how to prepare for that which is to come.

"I gathered that the experience of Mr. and Mrs. Wakefield, the only Europeans whom we found at Ribe, was in accordance with my own observation, and that they were quite willing to carry out any plan which might be approved by the directors of their Society at home for organising their converts into a civilised industrial community.

"I ventured to communicate to these gentlemen the impressions made on me during my brief visit, and the suggestions which some experience of life in the tropics enabled me to offer. Meantime, till the number of European missionaries is increased, only a very few liberated slaves can be made over to their care; but the position is quite one of the best which could be selected for a free settlement, in the neighbourhood of an important seaport, and of established lines of communication along the coasts as well as into the interior.

"I would suggest that the Consul be empowered to aid in acquiring any plots of land in the neighbourhood of either Mission, which may be required to receive any liberated slaves. I do not anticipate the slightest difficulty and very little expense in doing this; but it is a work in which the Consul should, I think, take a part, and the medical officer attached to the Consulate might usefully accompany his chief, and be consulted regarding many of the arrangements.

"I saw at these stations, as elsewhere in East Africa, much which leaves on my mind the impression that the insalubrity which is now ascribed to the climate is often due to a neglect of sanitary rules, which would cause similar results on any part of the coasts of India; and I, everywhere in Eastern Africa, found Europeans living in positions and under circumstances which any medical officer of ordinary experience in Indian cantonments would pronounce to be incompatible with healthy existence."

After some suggestions regarding the medical staff required for the Consulate at Zanzibar, the Report proceeds:—

"Much has been said at Zanzibar and elsewhere regarding the small number of actual converts, especially at the Church Missionary station; but it seems to me that, apart from their literary labours, if judged only by the character they have established among the people around them, Mr. Rebmann and his fellow-missionaries have neither lived nor laboured in vain. They seemed to me to be regarded as beneficent superior beings, whose presence the simple tribes around were glad to secure, and whose precepts and example they would gladly follow. Everywhere the leading men of the petty tribes welcomed us after their fashion, and more than once asked why we did not stay, with no apparent notion beyond the belief that we belonged to the same race, and had the same objects as the missionaries. One of them, however—a very intelligent petty chief at Rabbai, near Kissoludini—gave, as his reason for wishing us to stop, that 'more missionaries would be a protection against the two greatest evils they feared—the inroads of the fierce cattle-lifting Masai, and the efforts of the coast people to make slaves of the Wanika, who had hitherto maintained comparative immunity from the inroads of slave-hunters.'

"I may remark, once and for all, that Christian missions present to the civil administration in East Africa none of the political difficulties with which we are familiar in India. Educated Muhammedans do not sympathize with the missionary; but, except slave-dealers, they will not oppose him, and the bulk of the African Moslem, who are very illiterate, are by no means averse to listen to him. By the Negro, free or slave, he is everywhere regarded as a friend. The African is surprised to be told that the Great Spirit is not in a state of epicurean indifference to mundane affairs, and he is quite incredulous as to the non-existence of the apparatus of witchcraft and good and evil spirits, by which he believes the world to be governed. As a rule he is a materialist and positivist of the most practical character; but he has not the slightest objection of any kind, moral or material, political or social, to the missionary, whom he regards as a very amiable and inexplicable, but in many ways most useful, enthusiast, whom he is glad to welcome as doing him good in many ways, and greatly adding to the comfort and importance of the tribes in the midst of which a mission station is established.

"It will be seen that, of the eight places specified above as desirable positions for establishments of liberated slaves, four only are occupied:—

"Mombassa (Church Missionary Society and Methodist Free Churches);
"Near Pangani River, Magila (Universities' Mission);
"Near Kingani River, Bagamoyo (French Mission);
"Dar-es-Salaam, proposed to be occupied by the Universities' Mission.
"Whilst four remain to be provided for, viz.:—
"(1.) Near Port Durnford, or some other point as far north as possible between Lamoo and Warsheek.

"To this part of the coast slave-dhows running north are generally obliged to resort for water. There is also a considerable local demand for southern slaves among the Somalis, where they fetch a higher price than at Muscat, and from 2000 to 4000 are said to be taken annually. High-priced Galla and Abyssinian slaves are also often exported. Nothing is likely so effectually to check this traffic as a free settlement, under resident European superintendence—the farther north the better. Port Durnford is an excellent harbour, easily accessible, and is said to be a peculiarly healthy place; but the best spot can only be decided on after a careful examination of the coast by the person who is to have charge of the settlement. This remark is generally applicable to the other three places named.

"(2.) A settlement near Kilwa, which would act on one of the principal slave routes, and on the great port of slave export trade of Zanzibar. I have no doubt a comparatively healthy spot might be found on the sea-shore in the neighbourhood, from which a position might subsequently be taken up further inland.

"The same may be said of the other two spots named, viz. :—

"(3.) Near Lindy, or some other of the ports north of the Rovuma; and

"(4.) South of the Rovuma, as near as possible to the Portuguese frontier.

"The object of all these settlements should be to form a basis, whence it may be possible to carry out Dr. Livingstone's original idea of acting on the Slave Trade from the interior. I found that all the persons best acquainted with the coast and the Slave Trade were convinced that it is only from the interior that any extensive and permanent effect can be produced on the slave-hunting ground.

"No one seemed to doubt the essential soundness and feasibility of Dr. Livingstone's plans; but all agreed that a good and permanent base on the sea-coast was an essential preliminary, and this it need not take long to establish.

"The Universities' Mission has never, I believe, given up the hope of resuming this part of Bishop Mackenzie's plan, and one or other of the four places I have named is very likely to be taken up by them. For the others, I would trust to the efforts of private individuals or missionary societies: for I believe a very considerable extension of missionary enterprise on this coast may be confidently looked for.

"The same may be expected of commercial enterprise; and in the event of any respectable European setting up on the coast a plantation like that of Captain Fraser or Mr. Sunley, I would authorize the Consul to deal with him as with a mission, always remembering the less permanent character of his establishment. (Sometimes it might be desirable to have a separate Government 'shamba' or plantation, but I would avoid this if possible, so that the status of the liberated slave might, as nearly as possible, resemble that of an ordinary freed man, with the additional protection which he derived from being registered as under British protection.

"I have suggested no separate establishments to be formed by Government, from a sense that Government could not do the work so well or so cheaply as the missionary societies or private individuals. But Government should contribute effective pecuniary aid; and I would beg attention to what is said by Père Horner,* as indicating what may be considered the reasonable expectations of one of the best-informed and best-organised of the existing institutions.

"I would authorize the Consul to contribute whatever he may consider a reasonable amount, in every case in which the Consul may avail himself of the agency of a missionary society, or of any private establishment, to take charge of children, or of adults who are not in a condition at once to earn their own livelihood.

"Under no circumstances should anything be allowed to be paid into any British Treasury for the services of a liberated African, either on the ground of paying for his outfit or on any other pretence whatever. I have no doubt that it was a misunderstanding of the reason for some repayment of expenses of clothing and keep which gave rise to the misrepresentations regarding the disposal of liberated slaves at Seychelles and elsewhere. When a liberated slave is 'assigned' to a planter, who pays so many pounds for his keep and clothing before he was assigned, it is difficult for either the slave or the bystander to understand that the liberated slave's services have not been sold as really and effectually as if the money had been paid to the slave-owner before the man was freed."

Neither, I may add, in passing, should the system followed I believe by most Roman Catholic Missions of purchasing

* Vide *supra*, pp. 50 to 58.

slaves for manumission by the Missionaries, be permitted. I have no doubt it was sanctioned with the best intentions, but it certainly gives rise to misrepresentation, and there can, I venture to think, be no question as to the propriety of that prohibition of the practice which is, I believe, strictly enforced in all Protestant Missions.

Besides these Missionary establishments, we found at Ibo and Mozambique a few Portuguese priests; but I could not learn that it was considered any part of their duty to attempt Missionary work among the Africans; and even if it were, their numbers are not sufficient to do more than conduct the religious services required for the Portuguese residents.

The latter remark is also applicable to the French priests who are found at Mayotte and Nossi Bé; but as far as their ability goes, I believe, they are active in missionary work. I was told that they had opened schools, and afforded religious instruction to Negro and Creole children, and that want of means and numbers only prevented their doing more.

At Majunga, on the west coast of Madagascar, we found ample evidence of the great results which have followed the labours of the missionaries of the London Missionary Society in that island.

Majunga is the seat of government and chief garrison of a district conquered about forty years ago by the Hovas, or ruling race, from the Sakalavas. It is on the shores of Bembatuka Bay, a large inlet into which flow several rivers, including one which is navigable to within a short distance of the Hova capital of Tananarivo, where the queen resides.

There was no English Missionary at Majunga, when we visited it, nor could I hear of any one having been there for a long time past. All that we saw seemed to be originated and directed entirely by native agency.

Nothing was volunteered by the Hovas in the shape of information, nor was the subject of religion broached by them. We found accidentally that they had two large churches, and, having attended the morning service at one of them, we were told as the reason of the large congregations which we saw that "Christianity being now the religion of the Hova Government, most Hovas and many of the subject Sakalavas attended church and were regularly instructed."

The Sabbath was observed with great strictness, no work or trade of any kind being permitted to be done on that day by any of the natives or Banian merchants in the town.

The churches were large airy mat buildings, capable of holding from three hundred to five hundred people, built on a uniform and convenient plan. The large congregations which more than filled them were, in about equal numbers, men and women, extremely attentive to a long service, which resembled in its general features a Scotch Presbyterian service; nothing could be more earnest and devotional, orderly, and free from the slightest appearance of extravagance or rant. Altogether the impression left on our minds was that the great body of the Hovas at Majunga and many of their Sakalave subjects were at least outwardly Christians—that many of them were very earnest and devoted, and that Christianity had here taken root as the national religion, maintained and ordered in all its formularies by the people themselves without foreign aid or intervention.

From what we then witnessed and heard, I see no reason to doubt the accuracy of the description given in a late number of a well-informed Indian journal,* that there are in Madagascar "half a million of professing Christians, that twenty thousand children are at school, that there are some seven hundred churches, that the Bible has been translated and many books written in Malagasy, and that above a hundred and fifty thousand books in that vernacular are sold every year. Besides building their own churches and supporting their ministers, the native Christians maintain a hundred and twenty evangelists in the outlying districts. The Government has absorbed Christianity into its system just as Constantine did, after failing to stamp it out by bitter persecution. And this is the result of less than fifty years;- for although Radama I. allowed missionaries to settle in the capital, Tananarivo, in

* " Friend of India," Sept. 23, 1873.

1820, the faith was prohibited by Queen Ranavalona his successor, for half that time. A church that remained pure and increased under such horrors as those inflicted on it for a quarter of a century, and that maintains so many missionaries of its own, cannot suffer much from the political spirit which tries to use it for purely secular ends. As in all the purest churches of Europe, the work began among the middle and lower classes. Polygamy has been abolished and divorce regulated. Domestic slavery remains to be dealt with. The Church is teaching the people self-government. When Dr. Livingstone issues from his lakes and the task of doing justice to East Africa is fairly taken in hand, the Christian revolution in Madagascar will be so far accomplished as to enable that island to aid in the good work."

To the places mentioned above (pp. 63, 64) as eligible for the establishment of fresh missionary stations, I would add the Comoro Islands, especially Johanna, where any missionary would find himself able at once to enter on a field of useful labour, especially if he possessed some acquaintance with Arabic, or experience of work among the Muslims of India or Syria. I am unable to account for the little attention these beautiful, healthy, and most interesting islands have hitherto attracted from the friends of our Missionary Societies.

THIRD LETTER.

Recapitulation as to work to be done on the East Coast of Africa.
Ideal pattern of a completely organised Christian Mission to uncivilised races.
Practice of the early Church in dealing with uncivilised communities.
Departure from that practice in many of the Missionary Societies of the Reformed Churches in the eighteenth and nineteenth centuries.
Adherence of others to the primitive practice.
Principle that in Christian Missions nothing should be neglected which is necessary to the organisation of a perfectly civilised Christian Society.

Necessary prominence of clerical element.
Branches in which lay element may be most useful.
Medical Missionaries.
A certain amount of medical training should be required in all missionaries.
Exclusively Medical Missionaries— their School and College Training.
Nurses.
Philologists and Scholars.
Teachers and Schoolmasters.
Printers.
Artisans, Mechanics, and Agriculturists.
Note—The " General Instructions" of the S. P. G. and of the London Missionary Society.

Such are the agencies at work for the conversion of countless myriads of African races lying between the lake region and the sea; of which vast population at least six millions are within easy reach from the East Coast, ready to trade, ready to learn; well-inclined towards the white man, and only too ready to follow his lead whether for good or evil; everywhere recognising the Englishman as the friend and protector of the negro race. In civilisation they are little advanced beyond the early inhabitants of Europe before Prometheus taught them arts or Cadmus letters; but the Negroes are peculiarly docile, and everywhere tend rapidly to assimilate themselves to any more highly-civilised race with which they may be brought into contact. They seem to need only such a basis of moral law, and such a bond of union as Christianity supplies, to knit them into orderly and progressive communities. At present there is nothing to counteract the action of the cold materialism which, teaching selfishness as the highest wisdom, isolates every man from his neighbour. This perhaps is one of the natural religions of mankind; but by counteracting the formation of any social ties or organisations higher than those which keep together a herd of bison, it is an effectual obstacle to anything like permanent civilisation.

Infinitesimally small as has hitherto been the infusion of vital Christianity into the vast mass of East African peoples, it has been sufficient to satisfy any impartial observer that Christianity contains within itself the one thing needful to give coherence to the mutually repulsive atoms of savage life, and to unite the innumerable scattered clans of the Negro race into nations progressive in all human arts of civilisation.

I will now briefly note the deficiencies which it appears to me should be supplied, with a view to rendering the organisation of the East African Missions more perfect.

This opens the question, what is the pattern of a completely organised Christian Mission, such as should be aimed at by our Church in offering the Gospel to uncivilised communities?

In a paper which I submitted to the Church Congress at Bath, in October 1873,* I stated the grounds of my

* See Proceedings of the Church Congress at Bath, published by Rivingtons, 1873. pp.

as a Field for Missionary Labour.

belief that, in dealing with uncivilised nations, we have no warrant of apostolic example for confining our missionary efforts to sending out preachers and teachers merely of dogmas and religious doctrine.

The records we possess in the canonical Scriptures, give details of missionary work among civilised communities only. We know little of how the Apostles or their immediate successors organised their missions to really barbarous or uncivilised nations; but our oldest records of mission work among such people show that the earliest missionaries started with a band of fellow-labourers which, as nearly as possible, represented a completely organised Christian community, lay as well as clerical; and that as long as the Church continued to be a zealously active missionary church it was the object of all missionaries among uncivilised people to teach not only religious dogma and morals, but all the arts of civilised life.

This example has been but imperfectly followed by the missionary societies of our Church, since the revival of missionary enterprise in the eighteenth and nineteenth centuries. With some societies it has been a rule to allow of no expenditure of funds on any instruction but that which had immediate reference to religious dogma or morals. The principle has not been uniformly enforced, nor has the practice of missionaries always been in exact conformity with their instructions in this respect; but among our English missionary societies few have adhered to the early—probably apostolic—practice of making the Christian missionary a pioneer of material and social civilisation as well as a preacher of morals and religion; and when some individual missionaries of great eminence have devoted themselves to civilise as well as to instruct their savage disciples, their practice has been reluctantly tolerated and not unfrequently summarily checked by the ruling authorities at home.

Some of the most active missionary bodies in America have even gone further and sent out special commissioners to enforce on their missionaries the duty of preaching Christianity alone, to the exclusion of even such work as the education of the heathen, who came voluntarily to their mission schools for the sake of the secular education there afforded in conjunction with religious instruction.

On the other hand, others—and they are amongst the most active and successful Protestant missionaries—have adhered to the practice of the early Church. Their success in religious teaching among uncivilised tribes admits of no question, and seems to me to be generally in direct proportion to their adherence to ancient usage in this respect. I would cite the examples of the Moravian Church everywhere; of many, if not most, of the German missionaries, and of some Americans. The great success which has attended the labours of the Presbyterian missionaries among the educated Hindoos always seemed to me to be much connected with their attention to high education in European literature and science; and in estimating the causes of the wonderful results which have blessed the labours of the London Missionary Society in Madagascar and elsewhere, it is impossible to overlook the extremely practical character of the "General Instructions" given to the missionaries regarding secular as well as religious matters. "Our missionaries," the Secretary says, "are encouraged to go *all* lengths in the work of civilising and uplifting the peoples, and nothing is forbidden in that direction except *personal trading.* Our missionaries have built aqueducts, made tunnels, devised schemes for irrigation, and have taught the arts of tanning, printing, bookbinding, boat and house building, besides giving to many peoples a written language and a translation of the sacred Scriptures and of many other books."

I have ventured to quote at length in a note at the end of this letter, the "General Instructions" here referred to. Nothing can be more comprehensive or more spiritual than the "Instructions to the Missionary Clergy" which for a hundred and sixty-four years have been given by our own venerable Society for the Propagation of the Gospel in Foreign Parts for the guidance of the clerical members of their missions; but I submit that the general rules laid down for the management of missions to *uncivilised* people, in secular as well as spiritual matters, might go further, and might, without omitting a word of these old instructions, breathe more of the spirit of practical secular wisdom, as well as of fervent piety and self-devotion, which inspired the early missionaries to our land when they founded Iona and Lindisfarn, Croyland, Ely, or Canterbury, and which may be read in every page of the statutes of William of Wykeham and the great founders and foundation visitors and reformers of his age.

The Church of Rome has never favoured missions to uncivilised people on any other system; and, in the recent revival of such missions, the effects of not neglecting the elements of secular civilisation are everywhere noticeable, among the elements of the success which has attended what I have seen of the missions of that church in Asia and Africa.

I think the principle that the Christian missionary

should neglect nothing which is necessary to the organisation of a perfectly civilised Christian society holds good everywhere. But it is less obvious in the case of missions to civilised nations in India, China, or Japan, where there is little to teach in agriculture, arts, or commerce. Even there I think it would be well if our missions were oftener organised in the form of a complete Christian community, and less as a separate caste of theological teachers and preachers. But, in the case of missions to the wilder and more savage tribes, instruction in the rudimentary arts of civilised life should, I think, always be a part of the ordinary and uniform system of missionary work, and should not be left to be taken in hand or neglected, according to the views of individual missionaries. Nor should it be permitted to occupy too much of the time and distract the attention of the clerical members of the mission, who are especially set apart for religious teaching and for preaching the Gospel.

Nothing should be done to interfere with the position of the clerical element as the directing power in every Church mission. The secular elements of a civilised community should simply be added to such an extent as may be necessary for the daily life of a peaceable and well-ordered society. Arts necessary to this end should be taught by laymen thoroughly imbued with the missionary spirit, but limiting, as Churchmen, their own special work to the calling in which they are masters, leaving their clerical brethren free for the ministry of the Word of God, to the preaching of which they have been specially called and ordained.

I will now mention briefly a few of those branches of secular teaching in which it seems to me that the lay element may most usefully be called in, supplementing the labours of the ordained missionaries, to assist in the great task of a Christian mission.

Medical Missionaries and Nurses.—There are few more important offices in a perfect mission than that of the members who can undertake the regular and efficient discharge of duties as physicians and nurses, for which, as far as I am aware, no regular and efficient provision is made in most of our Church missions.

Much has been done to promote medical missions, but chiefly by bodies unconnected with our Church, and the Roman Catholics and our own Church at home have some excellent nursing sisterhoods from which many useful practical hints might be gathered.

Medical Training to be required of all Missionaries.—I do not think any missionary can be regarded as perfectly efficient, unless he has had sufficient medical education to enable him to deal with the commoner forms of accident or disease likely to be met with in the field of his future labours. Life and health are, I am convinced, often sacrificed owing to neglect of such training; and I would fix a certain course of study and attendance at lectures on the rudiments of medicine, surgery, and practical sanitary science, which should be demanded from every missionary sent out.

Some medical instruction is now, I believe, given at both our missionary colleges, at St. Augustine's (Canterbury) and at Islington; but what is specially useful to a missionary is instruction in at least the elements of sanitary science, in its more comprehensive sense. This is rarely accessible, and never as a part of regular and necessary training to even our best-educated parochial clergy, to most of whom it would be invaluable. Unless they have had a chance of attending the teaching of

Dr. Acland and his colleagues at Oxford, they are generally left to pick it up empirically and haphazard, probably as overworked curates, in the unwholesome streets and lanes of some crowded city; and invaluable opportunities of doing good are lost, and health and even life itself are often forfeited, in the process of learning. Sound elementary instruction on such subjects should be a part of all liberal and complete education; and such books as Miss Nightingale has written on "Hospital Management and Nursing" as well as on "Army and Municipal Sanitation in India and Europe," should form a part of the library of every missionary especially in the tropics.

Medical Missionaries.—But besides such general and rudimentary training as can be required from all missionaries, there should be in every mission a well-trained practitioner in medicine and surgery, qualified to practise and advise on sanitary matters affecting members of the mission, and also to make use of his medical skill, as an auxiliary to the mission work: following the example of Him who relieved all the physical sufferings of the afflicted as a preliminary to preaching the Gospel to them.

I would not require that all, who felt disposed to assist, should of necessity take orders, or bind themselves indefinitely to mission work. Much good might be done by even a year or two of active work from a lay volunteer who could not give his services for a longer period.

But though our societies might usefully encourage those who are ready to offer such temporary aid, it is still more desirable to train men, who could attach themselves permanently as medical members of a mission, and form a part of its regular staff.

The following suggestions with regard to the course of

study and estimate of expense of such education have been kindly forwarded to me by Dr. Theodore Maxwell, a member of the University of Cambridge, who is now in India as a medical missionary:—

"It is essential that a medical missionary should receive a good medical and surgical education; he should obtain a degree from a university, or a diploma from one of the licensing corporations in medicine and also in surgery.

"Four complete years is the minimum course of study prescribed by law.

"The Edinburgh Medical Missionary Society receive students into their institution (40*l*. a year being paid for board by each student) and pay the necessary fees to the university or College of Surgeons for their education. The students attend to *missionary* work at the society's dispensary in the Cowgate. The society is unsectarian. There are at present in the Institution, members of the Church of England, Independents, Baptists, and Presbyterians.

"The course I should suggest for a Church of England medical missionary is to go first to Cambridge or Oxford Universities, and then to the Edinburgh Institution.

"He must reside three years in Cambridge, during the latter two of which he should study medicine, or rather the introductory sciences, anatomy, botany, &c., passing the first and second M.B. examinations before leaving.

"If he is able to take an arts degree in honours, two more years in Edinburgh will suffice; but if not, he may not pass the final M.B. examination till he has completed five years of medical study, i.e. till three years after leaving Cambridge.

"He could, however, obtain a diploma from the Colleges of Surgeons and Physicians (which would suffice if time were an object) in two years after leaving Cambridge.

"As to expense—in addition to that borne by the Edinburgh Medical Missionary Society, it might be set down as—

	£
"I. Four years' board at Edinburgh Training Institution, at 40*l*.	160
Four years' clothing, washing, travelling, and personal expenses	160
Total for a student who does not go to Cambridge	£320
"II. Three years at Cambridge, everything included, at 180*l*.	540
Two years at Edinburgh Institution at 80*l*., excluding fees and books, given by the Medical Missionary Society	160
Total for a Cambridge and Edinburgh training	£700."

In another letter on the same subject to a friend at the Church Missionary Society's Institution, Islington, the same writer says:—

"I have just come home, after passing what I really hope is my *last* examination (Licentiate of the Royal College of Surgeons, Edinburgh). I am much pleased that some one belonging to our own Church is thinking much of medical missions. This work has, hitherto, been almost entirely in the hands of other churches. If a boy of sixteen or seventeen could get a scholarship of 50*l*. for four years, I should say—'Do not send him as apprentice to a surgeon—let him pass an arts preliminary examination, and begin at a medical school.' In four years (if he is 21) he could be qualified and could enter Islington for two years, which ought to be enough for him. The *best* thing would be to go to Cambridge for three years, then to Edinburgh or a London hospital for eighteen months or two years, and Islington one year. The *cheapest* plan would be to go at first to Edinburgh, where the Medical Missionary Society would keep him in their house (where I have just been), charging him 40*l*. a year for board, but paying for his lectures, hospital fees, and books. In four or five years he could take his M.B. and then go to Islington for a year or two. If a boy is good enough for a school exhibition he might get a scholarship or sizarship at Cambridge, and the Elland Society would give him 40l. if they were satisfied of his earnestness. There are two C. M. S. men at the Edinburgh Medical Missionary house now who would be much better at Cambridge for the first part of their course. If your friend has any funds at present at his disposal, he couldn't employ them better than by sending those men to Cambridge."

He goes on to speak highly of the Edinburgh Medical Mission House, but observes, that for a young member of the Church of England Cambridge has many advantages over a Scotch university.

In May 1870, the Rev. Canon Robinson wrote in reply to a plea for the appointment of medical scholarships in endowed schools:—

"We are in favour of providing, in all cases where the endowment will bear it, that there shall be exhibitions from the school, tenable not only at the universities, but at any place of scientific, technical, or professional education or study. By such a provision as this, 'Medicine' will stand on the same footing as the most favoured subjects of study. It will be open to the holder of one of the exhibitions, to use his exhibition while pursuing his medical studies either in a college or hospital, or as an apprentice to a practitioner.

"I anticipate that in the middle-class schools, where the training will not have any direct reference to a university career, a large proportion of the exhibitions may often be held by medical students.

"There will also, possibly, be some special scholarships in science founded in some places; these will also, in some degree, be in the interest of medical students, to whom the cultivation of science is a necessary condition of professional efficiency."

And again in July 1871:—

"As a matter of fact, the provision referred to is, I believe, made in every scheme yet published. But exceptional cases may yet arise, especially among schools of the highest grade, where the connection with the university is direct and immediate."

Such provision of medical scholarships and exhibitions in connection with Missions appears to be a subject well deserving the attention of our Church Mission Societies as well as of churchmen in general who are connected with endowed schools or colleges.*

Nurses.—Much more systematic provision should be made in all our Missions for attendance on the sick by means of trained nurses. The professional training in our own home institutions is probably equal to any in the world, but their connection with missionary bodies is only incidental, and never, as far as I am aware, so systematic or practical as may be found in all the Missions of the Roman Catholic Church. The sisters of that church who devote themselves to such work may, I believe, be divided into two classes: the one being nuns or professed permanent members of some religious order; the others being lay-sisters who devote themselves to the work either for life or for a limited period.

Philologists and Scholars.—There is one branch of secular training and work which has never been neglected by any of our missions, even by those who most strictly confine their missionaries to the work of evangelists and teachers; I allude to the study of the native languages, their reduction to writing, and the translation into them of the

---

* Much useful information on the subject of Medical Missions will be found in the pages of the "Medical Missionary Journal," a small periodical of which I have only seen a few numbers, although it appears to be now in the eighth year of its existence.

Scriptures and religious books. This work is so obviously necessary as a preliminary to teaching and preaching intelligibly to uneducated savages, that I here allude to it only for the purpose of pointing out that it is in its nature essentially secular work, and that it is work in which laymen may render valuable assistance to their clerical brethren. This seems a branch of work in which the Universities could very effectually aid by means of Travelling Fellowships or Scholarships.

Teachers and Schoolmasters.—The same may be said of the work of teachers and schoolmasters; but this has not been so generally recognised as a necessary secular adjunct to a Christian mission as the work of the philologist; and our societies sometimes place what seem to me rather injudicious restrictions on the expenditure of mission funds for educational purposes. As far as my observation goes, no sound educational work amongst uncivilised tribes can be considered as otherwise than a valuable auxiliary to missionary teaching, provided the teacher be a man of really missionary spirit, and that the great truths of Christianity are made an integral part and a necessary foundation of the educational course. This seems to me equally true of missions to civilised as well as to uncivilised nations.

Printers.—I would place the work of the printer in the same category, as a valuable missionary auxiliary in the conversion of civilised people, and as absolutely essential to making any great impression on the uncivilised. A small printing-press is an almost necessary adjunct to every mission on the East Coast of Africa. But all large work in printing should, I think, be left to the press already established with such success by Dr. Steere at Zanzibar, where a better press and more type are required—the work now carried on having already outgrown the appliances provided.

Many of the nations to which our missionaries are now called, have languages which are deficient in all the means of giving expression to moral truths or to abstract ideas of any kind; the popular vocabulary of such nations requires to be enriched by terms drawn from other tongues; the whole has to be reduced to written characters, and the results multiplied by printing—a task, in fact, has to be accomplished which has occupied some of the foremost nations of Europe for ages, reckoning from the earliest labours of pre-historical pioneers of civilisation, down to the invention of printing. Some of our modern evangelists have shown that all this course of reduction of language to written forms, its enrichment by borrowed terms, and the instruction of large masses of the people in its use, the composition of books in it, and their multiplication by printing, may be compressed into the term of a single life. Our missionaries are well acquainted with these facts, and generally act on them; but they do not seem to me to be sufficiently recognised by our parent societies at home. The task I have described is hardly regarded in our home committee rooms as a necessary branch of missionary work which may, indeed, be safely and suitably left to laymen, but which should in no degree be dissociated from the general and essential work of the mission.

Music.—The natives of Africa generally have a passion for music. Their own music is often to our ears very discordant and disagreeable—but they have very correct ears, keep admirable time, and are capable of being trained to a high degree of excellence as musicians after our European fashion, as we saw exemplified in the Choir of the English Mission at Zanzibar, and still more in an admirably-trained Band of the scholars in the school of the French Mission.

Artisans, Mechanics, and Agriculturists.—Next in importance, I would place the work of architects, engineers, and builders, of agriculturists, mechanics, and artisans, such as smiths, carpenters, masons, leather workers, shoemakers, millers, &c.

I have not a word to say against the practice of our missionaries when they endeavour to make themselves independent of the aid of such auxiliaries, so as to be able to live among the uncivilised inhabitants of Indian or African jungles, in the same simple fashion as the aborigines themselves live. It is doubtless necessary to complete success that a missionary leader should be able thus to live; but I venture to think it a still higher qualification that, while able and willing in case of necessity so to live, he should have at hand the means of instructing the savages around him in the rudimentary arts of civilised life. He must have the judgment to see when what appears to the European eye uncivilised, merely because it is simple, is, as will often be the case, really more effective than the civilised contrivances to which he has been used. An African thatch may be a better covering in an African climate than slates or tiles or iron roofs, and mud or mat walls may be for some purposes preferable to masonry; but he who is a master in his craft—and none but a master should be employed—will see where real improvement is possible, and be able to select from various native methods of doing the same thing, that which is best adapted to its end. The result will be a real advance in civilisation, leading to modes of life less animal, and to a gradual elevation of the missionary disciples in the scale of humanity.

How much laymen might assist in this work may be seen by a reference to what Dr. Steere and his brother missionaries have now to do on the East Coast of Africa. There is building, including a Church and Mission House; printing; teaching in many departments; cultivating land; some road-making; organising a hospital; and a variety of other work which the missionary must now do himself, if it is to be done at all. How effectual might be the aid which might be given him, if a few laymen, masters in the several arts required, would consecrate but a few months of their time to go and help him! They would find themselves none the worse when they got back to their usual field of labour in England, and might to their lives' end continue, in their several parishes, permanent and effective lay auxiliaries to the Mission with the working of which they had made practical acquaintance during the few months of their stay in Africa.

Steam launch.—Every Mission on the East Coast should be provided with a steam-launch, capable if possible of running up the shallow and tortuous rivers, and also of facing the open sea for a run of some days' duration. Such a boat will be found most useful everywhere, not only as a means of communication and locomotion, but as one of the best restoratives to persons suffering from fever or dysentery, and an excellent means of educating young converts to a calling by which they can always earn their livelihood, either as sailors or interpreters on board our men of war or merchant vessels visiting the coast.

I have said nothing of subordinate service; but no one who has observed how much the health and comfort of the community depend on the humbler lay brethren, who act as cooks, and hospital attendants, in a well-ordered French mission, will fail to see that the Apostle's illustration of the necessity of all members—however humble—to the completeness of the body, is as true now as in the earlier ages of the Church.

Reports.—Our system of drawing up missionary reports is capable of much improvement. They often contain most valuable information of every kind, mixed up with details of minor general importance in a manner which makes it very difficult to separate what is of permanent value from matters which are of very inferior or merely temporary interest. The American mission reports are often models for us in this respect. Their general arrangement is geographical or topographical, and the missionary information regarding each country, province, or district, is preceded by a brief and well-condensed notice of its area, population, characteristic products, &c. These notices are carefully corrected and improved from time to time, as fresh information is obtained—and useful maps are frequently added; so that the report of an American mission often contains, even in India, a better popular sketch of the geography and statistics of the district, where their missionaries are at work, than is acceptable in any other handy form. They are also models of clearness and fulness in the mode in which the missionary statistics and accounts are usually given in tabular forms, omitting small details which are not likely to interest persons at a distance.

NOTE.—The following are the "Instructions to the Missionary Clergy" of the Society for the Propagation of the Gospel in Foreign Parts alluded to above, at p. 72, as having been first issued at the beginning of the last century, and which have ever since formed the standing orders of the clergy of that Society.

"INSTRUCTIONS TO THE MISSIONARY CLERGY (1706).

" I. THAT they always keep in their view the great Design of their undertaking, viz. To promote the Glory of Almighty God, and the Salvation of Men, by Propagating the Gospel of Our Lord and Saviour.

" II. THAT they often consider the Qualifications requisite for those who would effectually promote this Design, viz. A Sound Knowledge and hearty Belief of the Christian Religion; an Apostolical Zeal, tempered with Prudence, Humility, Meekness, and Patience; a fervent Charity towards the Souls of Men; and finally, that Temperance, Fortitude, and Constancy, which become good Soldiers of Jesus Christ.

" III. THAT in order to the obtaining and preserving the said Qualifications, they do very frequently in their Retirements offer up fervent Prayers to Almighty God for His Direction and Assistance; converse much with the Holy Scriptures; seriously reflect upon their Ordination Vows; and consider the Account which they are to render to the great Shepherd and Bishop of our Souls at the last Day.

" IV. THAT they acquaint themselves thoroughly with the Doctrine of the Church of *England*, as contained in the Articles and Homilies; its Worship and Discipline, and Rules for Behaviour of the Clergy, as contained in the Liturgy and Canons; and that they approve themselves accordingly, as genuine Missionaries from this Church.

" V. THAT they endeavour to make themselves Masters in those controversies which are necessary to be understood, in order to the Preserving their Flock from the attempts of such Gainsayers as are mixed among them.

" VI. THAT in their outward Behaviour they be circumspect and unblameable, giving no Offence either in Word or Deed; that their ordinary Discourse be grave and edifying; their Apparel decent and proper for Clergymen; and that in their whole Conversation they be Instances and Patterns of the Christian Life.

" VII. THAT in whatsoever family they lodge, they persuade them to join with them in daily Prayer, Morning and Evening.

" VIII. THAT they be not nice about Meats and Drinks, nor immoderately careful about their Entertainment in the Places where they shall sojourn: but contented with what Health requires, and the Place easily affords.

" IX. THAT as they be frugal in Opposition to Luxury, so they avoid all Appearance of Covetousness, and recommend themselves, according to their Abilities, by the prudent Exercise of Liberality and Charity.

" X. THAT they take special Care to give no offence to the Civil Government, by intermeddling in Affairs not relating to their own Calling and Function.

" XI. THAT, avoiding all Names of Distinction, they endeavour to preserve a Christian Agreement and Union one with another, as a Body of Brethren of one and the same Church, united under the Superior Episcopal Order, and all engaged in the same great Design of Propagating the Gospel; and to this End, keeping up a Brotherly Correspondence, by meeting together at certain Times as shall be most convenient, for mutual Advice and Assistance."

The "General Instructions" of the London Missionary Society are not more comprehensive or explicit, as regards the conduct of missionaries in their clerical capacity; but they supply much sagacious and kindly counsel in secular matters which would not be misapplied, if addressed to the lay as well as clerical members of any Mission. They run as follows:—

"DEAR BROTHER,

"1. Now that you have been accepted for the service of the London Missionary Society, and are about to proceed to one of its fields of labour, it is with great pleasure that the Directors of the Society address to you a few words, expressive of their interest in your personal welfare, and their desire for the thorough usefulness of your missionary life. And to these they add a few counsels suggested by the Society's past experience, respecting the spirit in which your work should be carried out.

"2. The consecration which you have made of yourself to the Lord's service will, they trust, often be renewed. By your example, by the principle which rules your life, by your temper, by your diligence in work, and by your fervent preaching, may those who surround you, Christian and heathen, see that you are a living sacrifice, devoted without reserve, to your Redeemer and your Lord.

"As a minister of Christ may you 'preach the Word, be instant in season and out of season.' May you 'meditate on these things and give yourself wholly to them, that your profiting may appear unto all.'

"3. The educational training which you have enjoyed, has fitted you to enter upon the important duties which missionary life involves. But so great are the opportunities of usefulness which every sphere of the Society's work presents, that you will find no amount of acquired knowledge and no range of mental power too great for the demands which that service, in its higher forms, will continually make upon you. And the Directors urge upon you the careful continuance of former studies, that, as your years increase, your fitness may grow with them; and that so you may occupy a high place among the helpers of the Christian Churches growing numerous and strong in lands most heathen.

"4. Possessing mental and spiritual gifts, and having been ordained to the Christian ministry, you are now appointed by the Directors a missionary of the Society, and as such are attached to the Mission carried on in

The Directors also place in your hands the General Regulations by which the Society's Missions are now guided. And while they will be prepared to sustain you in comfort in the manner therein provided, they trust that you also will endeavour to rule your conduct and your public work in the manner which those Regulations prescribe.

"5. From the date of your arrival at your appointed station, you will become a member of the District Committee which has charge of that and other localities; and will be expected to co-operate with the brethren of that Committee in carrying out the range of work committed to their care. You will, however, not become a full member of that Committee, with power to vote, until you have been twelve months at your station, and have passed with credit the first examination in the native language (Regulations 7 and 75).

"6. The Directors suggest that, as early as practicable, you should make yourself complete master of all that relates to that field of the Society's efforts; the manners of its people; the early history of the mission; the plans which have been found most effective in instructing and elevating the converts; the measure of success which the grace of God has vouchsafed to efforts already made; and the position which the mission at present occupies.

"7. They urge you diligently to employ every available means of obtaining an accurate and intimate acquaintance with the native language, and not to rest satisfied until you have so mastered it in its structure and idioms, as to be able to use it in intercourse with the people, in a manner pleasant to yourself, and acceptable to them. After a time you will be expected to offer yourself for a series of examinations in the language, for which the Local Committee will make arrangements, and the result of which they will report to the Board.

"8. All general arrangements as to your work from the outset, and especially when your knowledge of the people and of their language will enable you to take a more prominent share in the public duties of the mission, the Directors leave to the decision of your brethren in consultation with yourself. They need therefore only to urge upon you ever to bear in mind the great purpose for which you have been appointed a missionary. You have been sent, first of all, to preach Christ, in all the purifying and elevating influences of His Gospel, to the people by whom you will be surrounded. May the power of that Gospel ever so deeply affect your own heart, that you may be daily impelled by ardent zeal for God to make known the Saviour whom you serve, that thus your highest work may be your chief delight.

"9. The relation which you will sustain to the mission churches involves questions of the highest importance. On this point the Directors have spoken fully in the SECOND PART of the Regulations referred to, and they invite your careful attention to their views. They do not wish you to be, except for a time, the pastor of a native church. They look upon you and your brethren as advisers and helpers of these churches, by whom they may be stimulated in that course of training which shall end in making them self-reliant, active, earnest Christians, supporting all the ordinances of the Gospel, and carrying its work onward to the ignorant beyond them.

"10. In connection with these efforts they would press upon you the importance of promoting education, especially among the young; that, by means of schools, you and your brethren may lay a firm foundation for future progress, and thus prepare the way for an intelligent appreciation of the great truths which make wise unto salvation, as well as for the better discharge of the daily duties of life.

"11. In conjunction with and subsidiary to these departments of labour, they suggest that any medical and surgical knowledge which you have acquired may often be employed as a means of conciliating heathen people; trusting that you will always so employ the wider access to the people which you may thus gain, as to point them to Him who is the great Physician of souls.

"12. In regard to your general conduct the Directors observe, that apart from that formal instruction, by which you will exercise great influence upon the people around you, you will have much power as an EXAMPLE. They, therefore, urge you carefully to watch, that that example be of the highest kind. In illustration of their meaning they offer the following practical hints, which you will find to be specially applicable to the position and circumstances in which you are about to be placed.

"*a*.—BE ORDERLY. Cultivate system in your daily

work and general plans. Cultivate punctuality in appointments of duty; in all payments of money; and in your system of public accounts.

"*b.*—BE THE CHRISTIAN GENTLEMAN. In the absence of European eyes, and amid the discomforts of tropical life, there is danger of losing something of the Christian civilisation in which you have been trained, and of sinking into careless and slovenly habits of dress and home life. You cannot, however, do this without injury to your influence.

"*c.*—BE SELF-DENYING. Natives are shrewd observers, and readily detect inconsistencies in those who are their professed teachers. Avoid display and self-indulgence in your style of life; in your dress; in the food and furniture of your house; and in your personal habits. Rather promote self-denial in those around you, by your own simple and self-denying practice.

"*d.*—BE THE STUDENT. The man who is compelled to hold constant intercourse with uninformed and uncultivated intellects, is in danger of indifference to his own mental culture. Earnest study of special subjects you will find to be a stimulus and a pleasure. Strive to maintain your own mental activity, and you will draw the people after you. Some of your predecessors have found it an excellent plan to adopt some special study as a relaxation from the usual routine of missionary life.

"*e.*—BE VERY PURE IN THOUGHT AND ACT. Surrounded by people of gross habits and language, try to educate them in purity, not only in word, but especially by example. Be watchful at all times over your conduct towards native women. By treating them with marked respect you will help to secure to them a new position in the esteem of their community.

"*f.*—CULTIVATE PERSONAL GODLINESS. Dread an official piety. Feeling the danger which is common to all Christians, strive most prayerfully to maintain and grow in genuine principle. For this end be diligent and regular in the study of God's Word for your own good.

Watch against weaknesses and 'besetting sins.' And pray much for strength and growth in grace.

"*g.*—BE PATIENT. Be watchful against an irritable temper. A hot climate, and frequent worry, will tend to promote such a temper; therefore with the greater danger let there be greater care.

"*h.*—AVOID HASTY DECISIONS. Pause over all important cases: pray over them: sleep over them. A hasty decision may prove a thorn in your hand for many years: it may be quoted most annoyingly as a precedent; and may be a trouble to your brethren elsewhere.

"*i.*—ENCOURAGE INDUSTRY AND LAWFUL COMMERCE IN YOUR PEOPLE, but do not become personally involved in trading transactions; and have nothing to do with land. Great trouble, loss of influence, and injurious collision with the people, will almost certainly result from neglect of this warning. While helping the natives by suggestions, keep your own hands perfectly free.

"*j.*—Do not allow yourself to be mixed up in NATIVE POLITICS. Do not in any way accept civil office. Advise, suggest; and by advice you may help the people greatly. But do no more.

"*k.*—Do not ANGLICISE YOUR CONVERTS. Remember that the people are foreigners. Let them continue as such. Let their foreign individuality be maintained. Build upon it, so far as it is sound and good; and Christianise, but do not needlessly change it. Do not seek to make the people Englishmen. Seek to develop and mould a pure, refined, and Christian character, native to the soil.

"*l.*—Remember again the NOVELTY OF YOUR POSITION, the difference in the habits and requirements of the people from those in England; and your comparative ignorance about them. Therefore pay deference to the judgment of your seniors as to what is best for them. Learn from the experience, successes, and failures of your brethren, and thus escape the bitterness of learning from your own failures.

"*m.*—Within the sphere of your mission, you may have

many colleagues. UNITE heartily in counsel and plan with your brethren when there is opportunity for so doing. Separateness of action always involves and insures weakness. To differ widely in plans from the brethren around you, will cause perplexity to your people, and often prove a hindrance to progress. Be ready to concede a little for the sake of common action.

"*n.*—PAUSE FOR EXPERIENCE BEFORE YOU BEGIN TO TRANSLATE. Knowledge is necessary to correct and idiomatic translation; and much time and trouble may be saved by not being hasty in undertaking this work. When you begin to translate, be accurate both on the side of the original and of the native idiom. Do not mind being slow for the sake of accuracy.

"*o.*—BE HONEST AND CANDID TO US RESPECTING YOUR WORK: help us to understand it by faithfully reporting its dark as well as its bright features. Do not exaggerate the good, nor conceal the bad: that while we rejoice in your successes, we may sympathise truly with you in your trials. Be assured that the Directors are prepared to offer you such sympathy in all your difficulties: and that they take a deep interest in everything which affects your personal happiness and the progress of your labours.

"13. With these practical counsels, which they offer only with a view to promote your comfort, and to aid you in your work, the Directors affectionately commend you to God, and to the word of His Grace. May the Lord be your helper, teacher, and guide. May He preserve you from all evil. May He deliver your soul from death, your eyes from tears, and your feet from falling. May He give you power as His ambassador. May He abundantly bless your work and message. May He grant you a happy missionary life, and make great use of you in His cause.

"On behalf of the Directors and of my colleagues,

"Believe me, affectionately yours,

"*Foreign Secretary.*"

FOURTH LETTER.

Means of supplying what is wanted by Missions in Eastern Africa.
Terms of Engagement for Missionaries, clerical and lay.
Question of Celibacy of Agents employed.
Objection on score of Expense: Answered.
Selection of Agency.
Connection of each Mission with special localities in our own country.
Raising of Funds.
Connection of Missions with University Life, and studies of Churchmen.
Example—Study of Semitic Languages.
Canon Westcott's suggestions.
Direct connection between misbelief or unbelief in Christendom, with the varying forms of Religion and Philosophy in Heathendom.
Aid to be derived from India.
C. M. S.'s African Orphanage at Nassick. Free Church Institution, Bombay.
General Missionary Library in England.
Co-operation of different Missionary Societies in this and similar undertakings.
Application of principles above stated to Missions in East Africa.
Opinions of Dr. Steere.
Conclusion.

I have endeavoured to show that for a field of labour such as is presented by Eastern Africa, where so much of the work lies among people more or less uncivilised, the Church should endeavour to send, not merely a few clergymen with a schoolmaster or two, but a body of men, laymen as well as clergy, under a qualified leader, representing as completely as possible all the elements of civilised society, with master craftsmen and foremen artificers, capable of instructing the natives in all those arts of civilised life which they now know not at all, or but imperfectly.

Before considering how what is wanted can be supplied,

it is to be noted that such an admixture of the lay and secular element as is recommended, necessarily implies some modification of the terms under which the missionary societies at present usually engage their agents, and which in the case of the clergy often imply, if they do not actually stipulate for the devotion to missionary service of the whole working days of the missionary's life. For laymen certainly, and I think for clergymen also, it seems very advisable that the terms of positive engagement should be shorter, and that the provisions of the engagement should recognise the truth that there is no essential difference between the service of the Church at home and abroad.

At present there is a vague, unavowed feeling in the minds of many Churchmen that mission work among the heathen of foreign lands is something essentially different from mission work among the untaught and irreligious of our own country—that it is a work of greater trials and privations, but needing a rather inferior class of mind and less educational training than pastoral work in our own country; and that a man may do very well as a foreign missionary who would not be considered fit for any but the lower grades of work in the Church at home.

I need not argue against impressions which, though they may influence action, rarely now take the form of opinions held or avowed by thoughtful or influential men; but these impressions, no doubt, are the result of opinions decidedly held, avowed and embodied in the records of our societies in days gone by, and which have left their impress on the terms which our societies are in the habit of still offering to the missionaries they engage, and also on the feeling with which, and the classes by whom foreign missionary work is often undertaken.

If the Church generally recognised the fact of the great similarity between the work to be done in the darkest regions of heathendom and the neglected districts of our own country—that, as in Europe, so in foreign heathendom, there is no talent so great but that it may worthily be employed in the Church's service, no talent so small that it can be superfluous or useless in aiding the work of the Church—we might hear less of the difficulty of getting men for the work; it would less often appear to be the work of a class or a clique, and would more clearly be seen in its true proportions as the noblest work that can be intrusted to man. I shall have occasion further on to quote the opinion of Dr. Steere as to the great service which might be rendered to missionary work in East Africa, by visits from earnest and zealous men, who cannot give more than a year or two to the foreign service of the Church; and I would only now observe that I do not in the least undervalue the superior efficiency of lifelong devotion to one line of labour, and I have no doubt that such devotion will often be the result of labour undertaken with a more limited object in view. The work itself, if undertaken in a proper spirit, will be its best earthly reward; and, with this conviction, I would make the term of formal engagement as brief as possible.

Of late years, whenever increase of missionary agency is discussed, we are apt to hear the opinion broached that it is hopeless to expect such a supply of agents as the Church needs, unless under conditions of celibacy, such as admit of many men uniting for one object untrammelled by family cares or expenses; and this opinion is not unfrequently supported by arguments as to the superior intrinsic efficiency of celibate agency for Church purposes generally. I may be pardoned, therefore, if I offer a few brief remarks as to the comparative advantages of insisting on the celibacy of the agents engaged by our missionary societies. My own observation, as a layman, may not be of much value; but I feel bound to record my strong conviction, that whatever reasons our forefathers may have had for employing celibates in missionary work, the arguments of reason, experience and common sense, in these days are all in the other direction. Family ties in India or Africa, of course, as elsewhere, bring increased cares, and there is even more necessity than at home that the lay associate, who devotes himself to missionary work, should be cautious in the choice of his partner for life, and prudent and self-denying at least to the same extent as the young lawyer or physician, as regards the time when he will marry; but a very large observation of the class from which I should hope for most help, convinces me that, in the long run, something more than a double amount of good work may be expected during the lifetime of the man who has prudently married or who purposes so to marry, as compared with his professed celibate brother, and that the work will generally be better and more permanent if not more rapid.

The organisation and administration of a mission, in which many of the members were married, would, of course, be, in some respects, a less simple undertaking than that of a mission in which the celibacy of the members was insisted on; but the experience of many missions—notably those of the Moravians and some of the German societies —proves that the difficulties are neither insurmountable nor incompatible with the strictest economy of means or with conspicuous success of the mission.

Objection on the Score of Expense.—I would anticipate one objection which may be raised to the suggestions I have offered on the score of expense. There may at first be a considerable apparent increase in the expense of a mission if, in addition to the clergy, who alone are now provided by our missionary societies, lay aid is to be supplied in the shape of medical men and nurses, schoolmasters, artisans, and agriculturists; but I have no doubt that, in the long run, the system I venture to suggest will be found the more economical of the two, on the broad ground that it is bad economy to employ costly labour, like that of the educated clergy, on work which can be equally well performed by less highly-trained, and therefore less costly, agency. It is well that the clerical head of a mission should know how all these things are to be done, and even be able to do some of them with his own hands, as an element of governing and directing power; but it is not sound economy when a man perfectly qualified for the episcopal direction of a large missionary see, is forced to spend much of his time as a master builder, or printer, or carpenter.

I think, too, by the system I have recommended there would frequently be a great economy of health and life. I can recall within my own experience many cases in which the presence of a good medical coadjutor would have saved the health or life of missionaries when stricken down by disease, and other cases where a medical missionary would have avoided the selection of localities for mission stations, and seasons of work subsequently proved inimical to health, by costly, and frequently fatal, experience.

It has often occurred to me, when considering the melancholy list of martyrs to their work in some missions, especially those of the Romish Church, that much of the mortality was due to the absence of domestic comforts and appliances, by no means incompatible with the most devoted missionary work. I would not for a moment reflect in any way on those noble martyrs who have given their lives in the hope of evangelising the heathen; but, as members of missionary societies, we are bound wisely to husband and apply to the best advantage the health and strength of our missionaries, as in the case of all other talents committed to our care, and we shall surely not be guiltless if we allow life or labour to be wasted which might have been devoted to the work of an evangelist.

Selection of Agency.—With regard to the mode in which the lay agency required should be selected, I would leave it as much as possible to the local head of the mission. As in the case of clerical members, so lay coadjutors will generally best be chosen by those with whom they are to work. There are probably few neighbourhoods in the United Kingdom where qualified recruits could not be found by careful inquiry among the middle and lower classes. The first requisite should, of course, be devotion to the mission work for Christ's sake; the second requisite, personal knowledge of, and personal affection for, the superior under whose immediate orders they are to do the work of their Heavenly Master.

Opportunities of enlisting recruits from all classes would offer whenever the leading members of the mission revisited Europe, as they should be encouraged to do from time to time, to raise funds and to enlist fresh members for the mission, both lay and clerical. Of course, no general rule on the subject is applicable to all cases; but, as far as my experience goes, the missions which are best supported with men and money are always those where there is least restriction placed on the visits of the leading officers of the mission to head-quarters, where they can plead the cause of their own mission, and obtain exactly the kind of aid, and choose the precise kind of men they require.

Of course, the privilege of doing this, like any other privilege, may be abused, and its abuse should be sternly checked by the Church authorities and the parent societies at home. But I have generally observed that where there is most vigorous life in the mission, it is difficult to move the directing head from the scene of his work, even when the most pressing reasons require his temporary absence. On the other hand, where a mission languishes for want of life among its members, the needful impulse may often be given by a requisition to return home and give an account of stewardship. England is, after all, the great heart and centre of our mission activity, and the more rapid the circulation between the heart and the extremities, the quicker and healthier will be the flow of life-blood and the more rapid the growth.

I believe that the success of missions would be greatly promoted, and the general interest in their progress would be considerably increased, if more care were taken to connect the missions abroad with particular localities in our own country. This has been partially done in a few cases with manifest success; but I think it should be attempted more on system. Every one who has attended provincial missionary meetings must have been struck by the extraordinary difference in the interest taken by the audience, when any of the facts stated related to fellow-townsmen or neighbours of their own; and there can be little doubt but that, if any of our large towns or metropolitan parishes were to agree to concentrate effort in the support of some one particular mission, it would be far easier than at present, not only to raise funds, but also to obtain men when required. This need in no degree weaken the connection between the missions and the great parent societies.

Funds.—As regards the mode of raising funds, I have in a previous paper on "Indian Missions" described the very simple and effectual plan by which large sums are raised for missionary purposes in France.* The incumbent selects from his parishioners those whom he thinks most zealous and efficient as collectors, and charges each to bring to the weekly offertory a fixed number of contributions from their friends, at—say 1*d*. each, marking separately on the wrapping paper any which are destined for any particular mission. When the collector finds that his contributors exceed the fixed number prescribed to him by his pastor, he selects one of his subscribers to repeat a similar process among his friends, and so on, as far as the available resources of the parish permit. A steady stream of small contributions is thus realised, capable on special occasion of expansion; and the whole is managed with no more writing or reporting than the incumbent's weekly list of sums contributed, and the missions for which they are destined, which he forwards, with the money, to the bishop, by whom it is paid over to the treasuries of the missionary societies. It is, in fact, a combination of a regular offertory, with systematic and sustained individual exertion in collecting.

It is probable that great life and energy might be imparted to advocacy of the missionary cause if, in each neighbourhood, many churches could combine to have the same cause pleaded before each congregation on the same day, as is done in some of the northern counties in England with regard to school funds, and as has been lately

* "Indian Missions." 2nd Edit. London: J. Murray, 1873; p. 82.

tried in London with regard to a Hospital Sunday. It always seemed to me an excellent feature in the north country practice regarding school funds, that the same cause was brought on the same day simultaneously before the several congregations, not only of the various parish churches, but in the places of worship of all other denominations to be found in the neighbourhood.

There is at present no direct connection between our Cathedral Chapters, and Missions, home or foreign. Might not a great amount of writing and reporting and a very considerable expenditure of money and time be saved if in each diocese the collection of funds for missions and church purposes were entrusted to an officer with a fixed and permanent residence, say, a member of the cathedral chapter, who would receive and convey to their destination and grant acknowledgments for the contributions received from each parish? Few things connected with our missionary societies in this country strike one more forcibly than the great waste of time, energy, and money which accompanies the collection of the contributions.

There remain some points connected with missionary work in this country, regarding which I may be pardoned a few observations. One relates to the almost total absence of any reference to foreign missions in the university life and studies of churchmen.

Universities.—I have elsewhere ventured to point out, that it is close upon two centuries since the founders of the Society for the Propagation of the Gospel in Foreign Parts spoke the mind of our English Church regarding her duties as a missionary church;* and that it is more than two generations since the Church Missionary Society

---

* "The Church of England, her Foreign Missions, and the Universities," in "Mission Life" for January, 1874.

gave practical expression to the light in which this, among other long-neglected calls to action, was viewed by the awakened consciences of churchmen; since then every movement in the Church, whatever its origin, has borne more or less testimony to an increasing sense of her missionary obligations. During this same period our universities have wonderfully expanded in every branch of national training, yet nothing has been done, as a part of our university system, to aid the Church in this branch of her duty; and it is still possible for a student to pass through the university course, and never to suspect that his national church had anything to do with missions, beyond treating them as a refuge for the less fortunate members of the two lower orders of clergy.

The omission can hardly be accounted for by the fact that our universities are no longer exclusively church institutions. The changes which have opened them to all comers ought rather to have the contrary effect. The same obligations, to obey the parting commands of our Lord, have been felt with increasing force by all other branches of His Church as well as by our own. Men like Dr. Livingstone, or Mr. Ellis, or Father Horner might now be class-fellows with such English churchmen as Bishops Selwyn, Patteson, or Mackenzie; and the additions to the teaching of the university, which would make students more efficient missionaries, are neither more nor less than those which would be equally needed to train them more efficiently as secular civilisers of mankind in distant regions as Indian civilians, foreign attachés, merchants, soldiers, or settlers, even if the teaching of religion were altogether ignored.

I would cite as one instance the study of Arabic and its cognate languages—a study which in itself or its results is of the utmost importance to diplomatists and administrators, to merchants and manufacturers, as well as to missionaries, divines, and philologists. There was a time when our universities afforded the best teaching in Christendom, as regards Semitic languages; and we have probably more to do with Semitic races than any other European nation. No libraries have such stores of Semitic literature as ours; but it can hardly be said that the Semitic teaching of our universities is proportionately comparable with the teaching and scholarship of some continental nations.

The subject of maintaining the old position of our universities as seminaries of Oriental learning has been very inadequately noticed hitherto by our university reformers, and I have no doubt that, if attention were once directed to it by your Grace and your colleagues, steps would be taken to place our universities in the same relative position that they occupied in this respect two centuries ago.

The following is the opinion of one who is perhaps better qualified than any living Englishman to give a critical opinion on the merits of modern Arabic scholars. He had been referred to on the subject of a missionary to be employed in Arabia, and he replied:

"As far as my experience goes, we have not a competent man available for such a post. The ignorance of Islâm among the English clergy is deplorable, and no man should be sent to preach the Gospel to Muslims who is not well up in their theology. Equally deficient are we in men having an adequate knowledge of the Arabic language, without which it would be useless to approach them, and Aden of all places in the world is the worst off for teachers. Any organised attempt to carry the Gospel into Arabia should be preceded by the foundation of additional Arabic scholarships either at Oxford, Cambridge, or St. Augustine's, where further professorships should also be established for teaching missionary students what Islâm is."

Dr. Rebmann, whose experience is greater than that of any missionary on the East Coast, considers Arabic so important to any one dealing with Muslims, that he assured me he would devote several years to its attainment, as a preliminary qualification for his work, were he permitted to live over again the lifetime he has devoted to missionary work in Africa.

The general subject of the relation of our universities to missionary work has, I know, attracted much attention from some of the most eminent men in the universities; and I venture to quote the following "Suggestions on the Characteristic Office of Universities with regard to Missionary Work," by the Rev. Canon Westcott, D.D., Regius Professor of Divinity at Cambridge, as indicating modes by which, in his opinion, the aid of our universities can be most useful to the great work:—

"There are two main lines in which it appears that the universities can assist in furthering missionary work:

"I. By providing or training men to take part in it.

"II. By literary co-operation with missionaries.

"I. With regard to the supply of men for missionary work, two distinct classes must be considered:

"1. Ordinary students in the university.

"2. Students elsewhere who already contemplate mission work.

"1 (a) There can be little doubt from the experience of last December that the claims of Missions can be brought effectively before members of the university by some general service and meeting (held perhaps annually), which shall include special devotional exercises and notices of definite openings in the Mission field.

" (β) There is also good reason to believe that some among the younger Fellows resident in the universities would be prepared to offer themselves for short periods of work ; and that their services might be of great value in the chief cities of India.

" 2. Students who are preparing for Mission work may be helped in two ways: (α) by exhibitions at the universities; and (β) by exhibitions tenable elsewhere.

" (α) It is unnecessary to dwell upon the peculiar advantages which the universities offer to men preparing for one of the most arduous branches of ministerial work. The expense of living at the universities need no longer be a hindrance to residence. It may also be worth while to consider whether it would not be wise to offer opportunities to native candidates for the ministry to pass some time in an English university.

" (β) It seems desirable to establish, as far as may be possible, some bond of connection between the Faculties of Divinity in our universities and the English and native pastoral seminaries already established.

" If such a connection should prove to be impracticable, it would still be desirable that the contributions of the universities in aid of Mission work should be specially devoted to the support of native pastoral seminaries.

" II. The literary co-operation of the universities may take different forms.

" 1. Popular professional lectures on special points of general interest, e.g. 'The Sacred Books of the East,' might be of considerable service to the cause of Missions.

" 2. It might be of advantage to consult from time to time with those actively engaged in Mission work on the issue of expository or controversial tracts to meet special wants or forms of objection to Christian teaching.

" 3. The experience of teaching on a large scale in the universities might be made available for the determination of a course of reading for native converts and teachers.

"It may be further asserted that Mission work among the Mohammedans appears to call in a peculiar manner for the kind of service which the universities are best able to render. I may add that, in at least one College in Oxford there is a Collegiate Missionary Association, the members of which meet regularly for communicating information regarding foreign Missionary work and for supporting a particular Mission in India. This seems to me a system worthy of more general adoption in our Universities."

With reference to Canon Westcott's concluding observations it may be remarked, that there is probably no form of misbelief or unbelief which troubles our parochial clergy among the neglected or ill-educated populace of our great towns, with which they would not be better prepared to cope, by attending a few series of lectures on some of the commonest sects and philosophies of the East. Forms of antagonism to Christian doctrine and practice, with which our English theologians rarely grapple in the shape of a regular system and school of thought, may be found by the student of Oriental religions reduced to order and enshrined in works of great repute. And many a fashionable but pernicious fallacy, which finds temporary currency among the loose thinkers of the day, will be recognised as an exploded Moslem heresy, or a tenet of some Hindoo philosopher, whose system has, ages ago, been shattered into fragments by Sanscrit controversialists.

Aid from India.—I have not noticed the extent to which missionaries and teachers who have served in India or among the native tribes of the Cape Colony can be useful in East Africa. The value of any practical acquaintance with the Zulu or Basuto language or customs is, of course, self-evident; but I was not aware, till I visited the coast, how widespread and powerful was the influence of the Indian traders, who everywhere monopolise the office of distributors of imports and collectors of articles of export for the foreign merchant. At all the ports which we saw, to the number of some two dozen, we found all trade passing through their hands, and they are the only capitalist class. They belong generally to one or other of the six trading castes already enumerated—Bhattia, Banian, Lohana, of the Hindoos; and Khoja, Bhora, or Mehmon, of the Muslims. All are well known to our Western Indian missionaries, and often to be found in our Mission and Government schools in the Bombay Presidency as apt and willing scholars. From hereditary devotion to trade during many ages, and habitual absorption of all their ideas in money-getting, even in their earliest infancy, and from their often leaving school early to enter the counting-house or shop, European education has perhaps made less impression on these castes than on others in India. Yet they have produced some men, like the late Karsandass Mulji, who, without being professed converts to Christianity, have exhibited a heroism and devotion to the cause of truth and purity which would have done honour to any Christian martyr of any age, and whose conduct may be distinctly traced to the influences of Christian literature and teaching. All have learned to value European education, and with all any one who understands Guzerati, Hindostani, or Hindi may converse freely, and easily read such records and literature as they possess.

Hence it follows that any teacher from a school on the coast of Western India between Kurrachee and Goa would be able at once to converse and teach and be useful among the leading traders in any port of Eastern Africa from the Straits of Bab-el-Mandeb to Mozambique; and, of course, through the traders, access is in due time to be had to the native tribes and their rulers, native or Arab.

There are also some missionary institutions in Western India which might be specially useful to the cause in Africa—such, for instance, are the Mission schools at Kurrachee, Surat, Bombay, and other ports on the coast, at any of which a pupil from East Africa, whether of negro or of Indian extraction, would find himself among people to most of whom his race would not be strange or alien, and where he would every day hear the languages of Africa spoken in the streets and shops.

Among the schools which would be most valuable in this way I would enumerate that of the Church Missionary Society at Nassick, a very sacred town of the Hindoos, near the source of the great River Godavery, about one hundred miles from Bombay on the railway leading to Hindostan and Calcutta.

The Church Missionary Society has had a Mission in this city for more than forty years; and one of the results has been the establishment of Saharunpoor ("the city of refuge"), a flourishing Christian village just clear of the suburbs, where, among other institutions for the good of the converts, is an African orphanage, the foundation of which was due to what is called a "happy accident" more than twenty years ago. Previous to this period Arab dhows were frequently captured by vessels of the Indian Navy, with slaves on board; and when the slaves were brought to land at Aden or Bombay the adults of both sexes were handed over to the police, and generally allowed to go their own way, whilst the children were disposed of among such of the inhabitants as were charitable enough to take them and were judged by the police to be sufficiently respectable to be intrusted with the charge. But no special care was taken in the selection of the recipients of the children, and they were as often Muhammedans as Christians; nor was any registry kept of the children nor of their subsequent history. Hence it was hardly matter for surprise that many of the poor savages, old as well as young, thus turned adrift in a foreign seaport town, fresh from the hold of a slave-dhow, ultimately found their way to the brothels and dens of vice which are always to be found in the vicinity of a great harbour. This attracted the notice of Mr. Forgett, the humane and energetic Superintendent of the Bombay Police, and he took advantage of a large capture of some seventy children to recommend to the late Lord Elphinstone, the then Governor of Bombay, that the children should be sent to Nassick, where he knew that the senior missionary, the Rev. William Price, would take every care of them. All these children were thus thrown on Mr. Price's hands, almost without his being previously consulted, and without his having any opportunity of taking the orders of the missionary authorities at home, who at first naturally objected to a diversion of missionary funds subscribed for the use of the Hindoos to an orphanage for African foreigners. It was, however, obviously impossible to cast off the poor children, and the result was the establishment of the African orphanage at Nassick. Mr. Price was every way equal to the occasion. The children, on their first arrival, were, of course, unmitigated little savages. But they soon improved under the judicious care of Mr. and Mrs. Price, and have since formed an orderly and well-instructed community, recruited occasionally by fresh additions of orphan liberated slave children. All are instructed in industry suited to their sex and capacity, all are taught in Maharathi (the language of the country) the truths of Christianity, and a few of the aptest are also taught English.

The boys are brought up to trades and easily find employment as masons, carpenters, smiths, &c., and especially as cart and wheelwrights; and the orphanage there has become the chief factory of the district for improved carts and bullock and pony carriages.

Some of the young people have gone back to Africa to the Church Missionary Society's Mission at Mombassa, where we found Mr. George David, his wife, and a few companions maintaining the character of educated Christians among the Wanika tribes, and likely, I trust, in a few years to become the nucleus of a free and civilised African community. Others have gone with Livingstone, and are the "Nassick boys," who have been so faithful to him. He was much struck with the Saharunpoor Orphanage when he visited it, in 1865, just before he started on his last expedition. He took with him several of the lads who volunteered to accompany him; and doubtless we shall find, among his letters and notes, some details of their conduct; but that they had faithfully adhered to his fortunes we know, from the testimony of Mr. Stanley. A second detachment of Nassick youths—of whom Jacob Wainwright was one—volunteered to go in search of the great traveller—the tried friend of their race,—and arrived at Zanzibar just as Mr. Stanley returned from his adventurous and successful expedition. These men were sent up with the supplies which Mr. Stanley forwarded from Zanzibar, joined Livingstone, and appear to have since been with him up to the time of his death, and to have aided their companions in bringing his remains to the coast.

I have recapitulated at some length what has been before published regarding the Nassick Orphanage, partly because it illustrates the excellent results of Christian and industrial training on average African children, under circumstances of previous treatment least favourable to the success of any attempt to improve them, but more because I would beg your Grace to press on the Council of the Church Missionary Society the vast amount of good which may be done to African Missions by maintaining the orphan institution at Nassick as a means of giving an industrial and Christian training to African children in a good tropical climate, and under conditions most favourable to their improvement, but at the same time not likely to unfit them for return to work and life in Africa. I know of no other place, in or out of Africa, where these conditions are so likely to be attained; and I would gladly see the Saharunpoor Orphanage maintained as a permanent adjunct to the Mombassa and other East African Missions.

Another valuable institution in Western India which has done and may do good service for East Africa is the educational "Institute" maintained by the Free Church of Scotland in Bombay, for the purpose of affording to the natives a good Christian education in English as well as in the vernacular tongues of Western India. Dr. John Wilson, one of the original founders of the Institute, who has watched over and directed its operations for more than forty years, has ever taken a warm interest in African Mission work, and has almost always had a few representatives of African races amongst its resident pupils—Abyssinians, Gallas, Egyptian Arabs, Copts, and Somalis as well as pure Negroes. Some who have been educated there have since become leading men in their own countries, in Abyssinia and Shooa, &c. I have reason to hope that the General Assembly of the Scotch Free Church, under the guidance of Dr. Wilson's veteran fellow-soldier, Dr. Duff, and Dr. Murray Mitchell, are likely to start a Somali Mission, to which the Bombay Institute will be a valuable auxiliary.

Missionary Library.—I may note, in passing, the serious want in England of a library of missionary literature, not confined to the works of any one branch of the Church, but illustrating the labours of the whole Christian Church in the missionary field, since the apostolic era. Some of our societies have libraries which fairly record the work of their own missionaries, and we are rich in libraries of general theology; but a student must wander in many libraries far apart, and even to other countries, if he would learn the whole story of Christian missionary enterprise in any one country of the globe, and ascertain, not only what this or that society of our own has done or is doing, but what share of the task is performed by the missionaries of continental Europe or of America.

Is it too much to expect that there should be either at our great universities or capitals, or at Lambeth Palace or at St. Augustine's, Canterbury, some library where the missionary student might learn what was done in past ages by the early missionaries of the Eastern and Western Churches, and what is now being done by the various missionary bodies of his own country, unconnected with our Established Church, as well as by the Roman Catholic and Reformed Churches of the Continent, by the Americans, by the Russo-Greek Church, and what is now going on to infuse new life into the old churches of the East, Greek, Coptic, Syrian, Arminian, and Nestorian? Where he might find the latest reports of all modern Missionary Societies, as well as the folios which record the labours of "holy men of old?"

If, in the formation of such a library of general reference for missionaries of all sects and churches, the representatives of all our great missionary societies could be induced to co-operate, under your Grace's general direction, one great step would be gained towards the formation of a body somewhat resembling the Board of Foreign Missions in America, at which men belonging to separate societies might be brought to confer on subjects of importance to all, but regarding which their common action need in nowise impair their perfect independence where separate action was desirable.

I feel assured that the most informal and casual communication and conference upon topics of common interest—such, for instance, as the perfecting of translations of the Holy Scriptures—would lead members of every mission to learn something of what others are doing, which would be useful to the common object they all have in view; and occasionally the opportunity might be thus afforded of settling amicably and speedily differences which now cause prolonged bitterness between separate societies—such, for instance, as the demarcation of fields of labour, a class of questions now often discussed for years with persistent acrimony, but which might probably always be adjusted by a brief personal conference, and reference to good and neutral maps.

Immediate wants of our own Church in East Africa.— I would, in conclusion, offer a few suggestions with special reference to the action of our own Church and its missionary societies on the East Coast of Africa.

As regards the Universities' Mission, it is by its position and constitution calculated to furnish the episcopal element as far as will be needed for some time to come for the whole of the coast, and to afford the means for further expansion whenever the work to be done shall require the formation of other sees. The selection of a wise and pious successor to Bishops Mackenzie and Tozer seems to me the first requisite to give fresh life and vigour to work which, as already stated, has been well begun.

On this subject I cannot do better than quote the following remarks of Dr. Steere, than whom no one has a better right to offer an opinion:—

"It seems to me that the proposal that any one nominated to our bishopric should first come out and see the work which will lie before him, is a very important one and very sensible. It is impossible for any one who has never seen work in a new country to form any adequate idea of it while at home. We are just now passing through a crisis which ought to terminate in a fresh burst of life and energy. We must not allow the question, What is to be done now? to be supplemented by a discussion as to what ought to have been done ten years ago. For myself, if only the men come out, I see no reason why a settlement should not at once be made in Bishop Mackenzie's old country—not the Shire valley, but the Manganja highlands. The road to them is well known and as traversable as African roads are apt to be. Of course, the expenses would be considerable, and we must have good men to go. The road is open, and"—

After noting the uselessness of further discussions of the past, Dr. Steere adds,

"while I am in charge here, I will do everything possible to insure their success, and so, no doubt, will the future bishop. We can easily find a landing-place south of Kilwa from which the shortest possible road to the Lake may be taken. The establishment of this point of departure is what I have myself often mentioned as the next step which I should wish to see taken. There is no reason, if the men are ready, why the advance into the interior should not take place at the same time. Meanwhile a great door is open before us here; the whole town is eager after English education of any kind, and most are disposed to look pleasantly at our religious efforts. We have made a very deep impression upon the minds of the townspeople, and the Hindis, finding us here, expect from us what missionaries have done for them in India, and seem half ready to yield anything we press for. The Indian traders of Zanzibar, it must be remembered, hold all the inland commerce in their hands, and, though they travel little themselves, all the travelling merchants are in their debt, and depend upon them for supplies; so that the Indian merchant in Zanzibar, Bhattia, Banian, Khoja, or Bohra, as it may be, is really a power at and beyond the great Lakes themselves. And these men are ready to pay any price we please, if only we will give them English teaching, and quite understand that our primary object is, and must be, a religious one. It is for these reasons that I am doing all in my power to get on foot a school in the old Slave Market; and the Banyans themselves look upon this as entitling us to claim some at least of the land as a gift from Likmidass (the leading Banyan), who professed his willingness, when Sir Bartle Frere was here, to give the land, and 7000 dollars besides, for the purposes of a hospital, or, *as they read it*, for some purpose beneficial to the community at large, as they all say our schools eminently would be. I fancy there would be great difficulty in raising funds to maintain a hospital; but as to the mere general care of it, if England can send us out some sisters, I think we could find them native helpers and keep it going better than any other instrumentality. The Indian Government might assist us in regard to medical help; and our party even on the Lake Neyassa would find good nursing and medicine here a very important strengthener."

He then mentions a lady to whom the Mission will for ever remain indebted for her heroic exertions, single-handed, to maintain the girls' school at Zanzibar, and suggests that she might induce to join the mission some of the sisters who are now associated with her in similar missionary works in England, and adds :

"A good schoolmaster, certificate of no consequence, or preferably uncertificated—if married, so much the better—please to send us as soon as ever you can find us'one. I am the only clergyman here now, and if I fall sick there is no one to take my place."

I have not the least doubt that if a Bishop were appointed, he would be able to collect an amply sufficient body of clergy, and lay helpers of every class, by visiting, before he went out to Africa, our universities and some of the great manufacturing towns — assembling the friends of Mission work, laying before them his wants, and asking for aid and volunteers in carrying out the work before him.

He need not confine himself to what may be needed for the Universities' Mission proper, i.e. for those who will be paid from the Universities' Mission Fund. He might appeal to the friends of Missions in general, and offer to take charge of whatever may be given either in men or money for the exclusive use of the Church Missionary Society and the Society for the Propagation of the Gospel; for I trust that both the Missionary Societies of our Church will speedily have Missions on that coast, where the former Society has hitherto laboured single-handed.

It may not be in the power of the Bishop elect at once to make use of all the aid that may be offered to him; but if he will note down whence it can be hereafter drawn, he will be able to obtain it by writing when he reaches the future scene of his labours. But it should, I think, be looked on as an essential part of his duty that he and his fellow-labourers should periodically revisit their native country, for the purpose of recruiting not only their own health, but their missionary forces.

Much unjust criticism has been bestowed by the enemies, and some that is not wise by the friends, of Missions, in reprobation of visits by missionary bishops and clergy to this country. I have not a word to say in excuse of the missionary who comes home for his own purposes, and whose heart is not in his work; but, as regards the missionary whose heart is in his work, I feel sure that the difficulty is more often how to get him to visit England as frequently as, for the sake of his mission work, he ought.

England stands to foreign mission work now very much in the same position as Jerusalem did in the apostolic age; and the men and the counsel which are needed are not to be got elsewhere than in England, nor without that personal labour and selection for which the best of letter-writing is but a poor substitute.

The Church Missionary Society has already reinforced their Mission at Mombassa by the return of Mr. Sparshott, and are, I believe, prepared to devote increased attention and larger means to their establishments there, and at Kissoludini, where the foundations have been laid for very extensive missionary operations among the Wanika Massaions.

The Methodist Free Churches' Mission at Ribe will also, I trust, be reinforced, and the work so well begun by Messrs. Wakefield and New carried on into the Galla country, where it is clear a great field is open to those who have the courage and self-denial to occupy it.

North of the Gallas, as above mentioned, it is possible the Free Church of Scotland may organise a Mission to the Somalis; but there is room on a coast-line of seven hundred or eight hundred miles in length for more missions than all Christendom could at present organise. The island of Socotra affords a field full of interest, and little known, though it was once the see of a Syrian or Ethiopic bishopric, and is close to the Red Sea routes between Europe and India, China, or Australasia.

I have said little, except incidentally, of slavery or the slave-trade, the abolition of which was the main object of the Mission to the Sultan of Zanzibar. This is simply because I regard the spread of Christianity as almost synonymous with the extinction of both slave-trade and slavery. It has this effect, partly by its direct teaching, partly by its bringing with it the seeds of civilisation and settled government. Politicians and diplomatists may make treaties, and sailors and soldiers may enforce them, but legitimate trade alone can free Africa from the trade in human beings which drains her life-blood. No natural commerce can flourish whilst slavery exists, and Christianity and Christian civilisation and enlightenment can alone extinguish slavery. This is no fanciful sequence, but one which we have often seen in former ages in Europe, and see now perpetually recurring in other lands. The traveller, the merchant, the missionary lead the way, as pioneers to settled government and freedom; but no Government can be so settled, no freedom so extended or permanent as in lands where the Government and people are Christian.

Apart from all minor considerations, there is no quarter of the globe whence the call for missionary exertion comes to Christendom with greater force than from Eastern Africa.

Other portions of the same continent are more rude and savage, and have perhaps more need of the humanizing elements of Christianity, but of no other part of Africa, probably of no other quarter of the old world, can it be said that its subjugation by a Christian power distinctly lowered the region in the scale of nations, and made it more barbarous than when first discovered by Christian Europeans. Nowhere else is this result so clearly traceable to systematic neglect by the Christian conqueror of our Lord's last command to His disciples. For three centuries and a half almost all the nations of Europe interested in maritime commerce have, in neglect of every precept and instinct of Christianity, taken their share in preying on the life-blood of Africa: this is no figure of speech, but is strictly and literally the truth, for everywhere in Africa, during the greater part of that period, the bodies of living human beings have been one principal staple of the African export trade conducted by Europeans. In many parts what Europeans thus did only rendered barbarism more barbarous, but on the East Coast they did worse, for they destroyed an ancient and probably progressive Indian and Arabian civilisation, which had visibly mitigated the savagery of the aboriginal negro races. Europe has thus more to answer for on the East Coast than in many other parts of Africa. Let us be thankful that in some respects the great debt appears there most capable of future payment; meantime the call to, at least, attempt its liquidation is but the more imperative.

I have barely touched on the fields of labour in Central Africa opened to us by the great missionary traveller, who has so lately given his life to the work. Exaggeration in estimating the effects of Livingstone's labours for the missionary cause is almost impossible, and there is no part of the wide regions he has opened to us which is not connected by direct trade routes with the East Coast. His work therefore has a special value for East Africa. The object for which he laboured, to Christianize and civilise the vast central region, is a step in advance, to be taken as soon as a further base of operations has been established on the coast. From the Straits of Bab-el-mandeb to the frontiers of our Cape Colonies, no missionary can work without in some degree promoting the aim which Livingstone had ever before him, in the visions of that hope which sustained him in all his wearying toil. It is for us to do what comes to our hand of the vast work; and his example will henceforth nerve all after labourers, whether the share of the task which falls to the lot of each be small or great.

What we saw in Africa confirmed the belief. I had always cherished, that there is nothing in the circumstances or the character of the African races to make us despair of their gradual improvement and elevation in the moral, the social, or the political scale. It must be a tedious and very gradual process, often wearying the most patient, and disappointing the most sanguine; but I see no reason to doubt the ultimate result. The most important of all the many elements in the change is

I believe the teaching of Christianity, and it is because I believe our own Church of England holds and prizes among her titles to our allegiance the marks of a truly Missionary Church—obeying, however imperfectly, the last injunctions of our Lord on earth—that I venture to address to the Primate of that Church these few remarks on the work to be undertaken in East Africa, sincerely believing that nothing more permanent can be done for the amelioration of Africa than that our Church should recognise the duty before her in those distant regions, and strive, by God's blessing, to perform it.

of the British India, & Cape Navigation Cᵒˢ..................

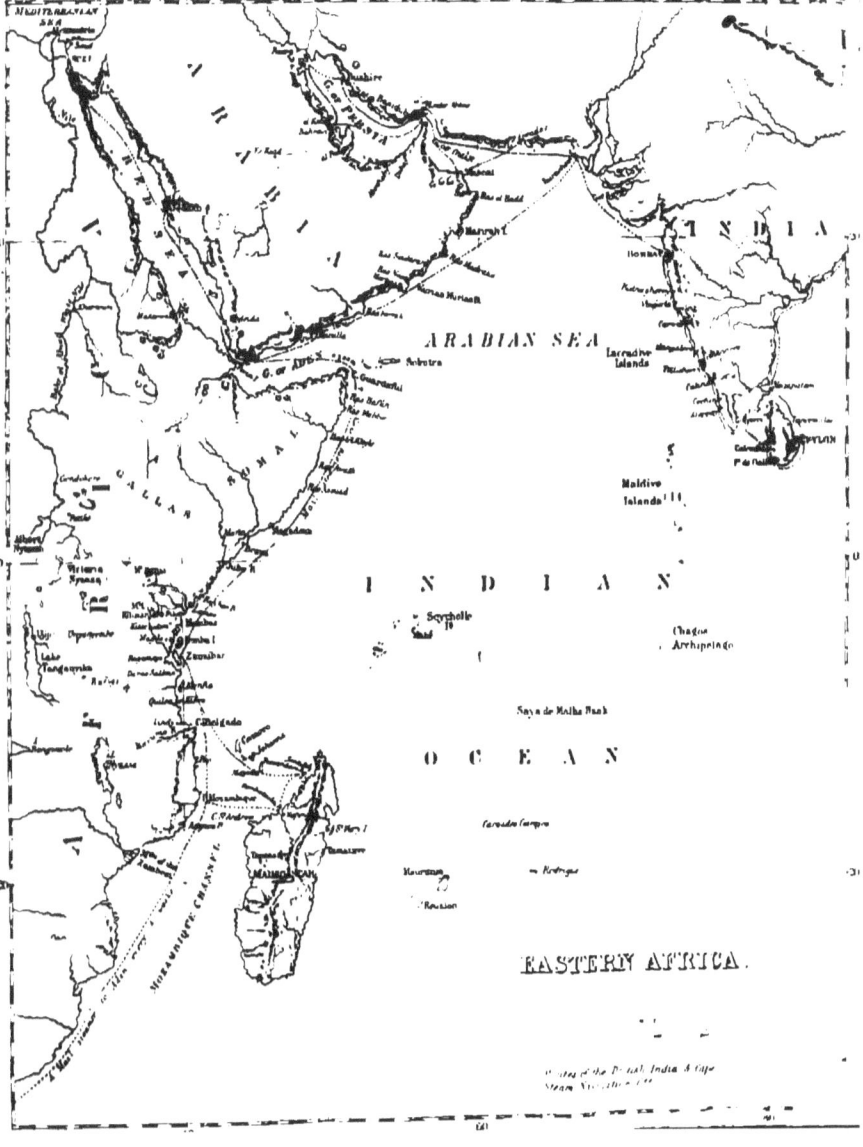

POPULAR TRAVELS AND ADVENTURES.

Consisting of Established Works, each complete in One Volume.

Letters from High Latitudes: an Account of a Yacht Voyage to Iceland, Jan Mayen, and Spitzbergen. By Lord DUFFERIN. 6th Edition. With 24 Illustrations. Post 8vo. 7s. 6d.

Nineveh and its Remains: Narrative of Researches and Discoveries at Nineveh during an Expedition to Assyria in 1845-7. By Rt. Hon. A. H. LAYARD, D.C.L. 12th Edition. With Map and 112 Illustrations. Post 8vo. 7s. 6d.

Nineveh and Babylon: Narrative of a Second Expedition to Assyria, 1849-51. By Rt. Hon. A. H. LAYARD, D.C.L. 6th Edition. With Map and 150 Illustrations. Post 8vo. 7s. 6d.

The Voyage of the 'Fox' in the Arctic Seas in search of Franklin and his Companions. By Capt. Sir LEOPOLD MCCLINTOCK. 3rd Edition. With 2 Maps and 30 Illustrations. Post 8vo. 7s. 6d.

Bubbles from the Brunnen of Nassau. By Sir FRANCIS HEAD. 7th Edition. With 13 Illustrations. Post 8vo. 7s. 6d.

Visits to the Monasteries of the Levant. By the Hon. ROBERT CURZON. 5th Edition. With 18 Illustrations. Post 8vo. 7s. 6d.

A Popular Account of Missionary Travels and Adventures in South Africa, during the years 1840-54. By DAVID LIVINGSTONE. 12th Edition. With Map and 32 Illustrations. Post 8vo. 6s.

[*Continued.*]

POPULAR TRAVELS AND ADVENTURES.

Five Years in Damascus, with Travels in Palmyra, Lebanon, and the Giant Cities of Bashan and The Haurans. By Rev. J. L. PORTER, LL.D. *2nd Edition*. With 18 Illustrations. Post 8vo. 7s. 6d.

The 'Rob Roy' on the Jordan, Nile, Red Sea, Gennessareth, &c. A Canoe Cruise in Palestine, Egypt, and the Waters of Damascus. By JOHN MACGREGOR, M.A. With Illustrations. Crown 8vo. 12s.

The Naturalist in Nicaragua. A Narrative of a Residence at the Gold Mines of Chontales; Journeys in the Savannahs and Forests; with Observations on Animals and Plants. By THOMAS BELT, F.G.S. With Illustrations. Post 8vo. 12s.

Life in Abyssinia; being Notes Collected during a Three Years' Residence and Travels in that Country. By MANSFIELD PARKYNS. *2nd Edition*. With Maps and 30 Illustrations. Post 8vo. 7s. 6d.

The Naturalist on the River Amazons; a Record of Adventures, Habits of Animals, with Sketches of Brazilian and Indian Life, and Aspects of Nature under the Equator, during Eleven Years of Travels. By H. W. BATES, F.L.S. *3rd Edition*. With 22 Illustrations. Post 8vo. 7s. 6d.

At Home with the Patagonians; a Year's Wandering over Untrodden Ground from the Straits of Magellan to the Rio Negro. By Capt. G. C. MUSTERS, R.N. With Map and 10 Illustrations. Post 8vo. 7s. 6d.

Five Years' Adventures in South Africa. With Notices of the Native Tribes and Savage Animals. By R. GORDON CUMMING. *7th Edition*. With 18 Illustrations. Post 8vo. 6s.

Perils of the Polar Seas; Stories of Arctic Travels and Adventure for Children. By Mrs. CHISHOLM. With Illustrations. Post 8vo. 6s.

JOHN MURRAY, ALBEMARLE STREET.

www.ingramcontent.com/pod-product-compliance
Lightning Source LLC
Chambersburg PA
CBHW020115170426
43199CB00009B/541